Cooking Around The World

INDONESIAN

Cooking Around The World

INDONESIAN

OVER 70 AROMATIC DISHES FROM THE SPICE ISLANDS

Sallie Morris

LORENZ BOOKS

This edition is published by Lorenz Books

Lorenz Books is an imprint of Anness Publishing Ltd
Hermes House, 88–89 Blackfriars Road, London SE1 8HA
tel. 020 7401 2077; fax 020 7633 9499
www.lorenzbooks.com; info@anness.com

© Anness Publishing Ltd 1996, 2006

UK agent: The Manning Partnership Ltd, 6 The Old Dairy, Melcombe Road, Bath BA2 3LR;
tel. 01225 478444; fax 01225 478440; sales@manning-partnership.co.uk

UK distributor: Grantham Book Services Ltd, Isaac Newton Way, Alma Park Industrial Estate,
Grantham, Lincs NG31 9SD; tel. 01476 541080; fax 01476 541061; orders@gbs.tbs-ltd.co.uk

North American agent/distributor: National Book Network, 4501 Forbes Boulevard, Suite 200,
Lanham, MD 20706; tel. 301 459 3366; fax 301 429 5746; www.nbnbooks.com

Australian agent/distributor: Pan Macmillan Australia, Level 18, St Martins Tower, 31 Market St,
Sydney, NSW 2000; tel. 1300 135 113; fax 1300 135 103; customer.service@macmillan.com.au

New Zealand agent/distributor: David Bateman Ltd, 30 Tarndale Grove,
Off Bush Road, Albany, Auckland; tel. (09) 415 7664; fax (09) 415 8892

A CIP catalogue record for this book is available from the British Library

Publisher: Joanna Lorenz
Senior Cookery Editor: Linda Fraser
Cookery Editor: Anne Hildyard
Copy Editor: Val Barrett
Designer: Siân Keogh
Photography and styling: Patrick McLeavey, assisted by Jo Brewer
Food for Photography: Jane Stevenson, assisted by Lucy McElvie
Illustrator: Madeleine David

Previously published as *The Essential Indonesian Cookbook*

1 3 5 7 9 10 8 6 4 2

Food has been an invaluable passport for me as a traveller on countless journeys to many parts of the world.
Malaysia and Singapore opened my eyes to the delights of oriental cooking which in turn led me to explore
and cook the foods from all over South-east Asia. I have indeed been fortunate in meeting so many people
who share my enthusiasm for food.
Janet and John Russell, ex Jakarta, were very helpful when I started this book. Beryl Castles M.B.E. helped
me enormously with the typing of the text.
John Phengsiri at Wang Thai supermarket (now Paya-Thai Market), 101–3 Kew Road, Richmond, Surrey,
TW9 2PN, 020 8332 2959, runs a wonderful shop where I have been able to buy all the ingredients required
to test the recipes.
Finally I thank my family, Johnnie, Alex and James, who with many friends have shared the rich delights of
Indonesian fare at our table in the past few months.
Sallie Morris

NOTES

For all recipes, quantities are given in both metric and imperial measures and, where appropriate, measures are also given
in standard cups and spoons. Follow one set, but not a mixture because they are not interchangeable.

Standard spoon and cup measurements are level. 1 tsp = 5ml, 1 tbsp = 15ml, 1 cup = 250ml/8fl oz

Australian standard tablespoons are 20ml. Australian readers should use 3 tsp in place of 1 tbsp for measuring small
quantities of gelatine, cornflour, salt etc.

Medium eggs should be used unless otherwise stated.

CONTENTS

INTRODUCTION

Visitors to Indonesia might be able to name just a handful of the more widely known and frequently visited islands, such as Bali, Java, Lombok and Sumatra, which are part of the fabled Spice-Island archipelago.

They may be surprised to know that the population of Indonesia now exceeds 185 million and is still growing, and is spread over 17,000 islands. What is more surprising is that only 4,000 of the islands are inhabited.

Over the centuries, waves of traders and merchants landed on Indonesia, in search of valuable spices from these lush tropical and volcanic islands. They left behind influences on the culture, religion, customs and, of course, cuisine. Indonesian food cleverly accommodates this rich tapestry of foods brought by migrants and traders over the centuries and today we can

enjoy the delicious kaleidoscope of tastes, textures and warm, spicy aromas of this fascinating cuisine.

Hindus in the first century and Buddhists in the eighth century left a legacy of vegetarianism, along with many beautiful temples; the most famous is the world's largest, at Borabodur, near Jogjakarta, in central Java. Islam was brought to the islands

by Arab traders in the fifteenth century and is the faith embraced by 85 per cent of Indonesians today. This should mean that pork is off limits but there are islands, such as Bali, where pork is elevated to festival food – and Bali has a lot of festivals, as we discovered on one of our visits there.

The next traders after the Arabs were the Portuguese, followed by the Dutch, who stayed for 250 years, until Independence in 1945. In addition, a steady flow of Chinese migrant traders, merchants and workers over the centuries gave another dimension to the richness of Indonesian cuisine and its warm and generous people. Sir Stamford Raffles, founder of Singapore and a one-time resident, wrote "By the custom of the country, good food and lodging are ordered to be provided for all strangers and travellers arriving at a village and in no country are the rights of hospitality more strictly observed by both custom and practice".

Rice is the staple food and it grows in abundance throughout the islands. The view from the air as we flew the length of Java was of hundreds of miles in any direction of lush green paddy fields. Driving along country roads on Bali – they are all "country" roads on this most exquisite island – we were captivated by the view as we rounded each corner: terraces of paddies, fringed with palm trees, which, away from the south-coast area of serious tourism called Kuta, had us almost believing that this was a little glimpse of heaven. On Madura, another island just north of Java, we spent a delightful sojourn.

Exotic fruit and vegetables are the order of the day at this colourful outdoor market in Denpasar, on the beautiful Indonesian island of Bali.

There, we had home-cooking at its best and I left the island with photographs and recipes which greatly enhanced and extended my knowledge of Indonesian cuisine.

Madura, unlike its neighbour Java, is about the same size as England, but it is rather dry and almost arid. Lack of rainfall is a problem; where other islands always get two and possibly three crops of rice, Madura gets one certain crop and, if lucky, enough rain just to sustain the second crop. The island has not as yet been "discovered" by tourism, though the bull races held during August and September rival those through any Spanish town. Heats are held in each district, with the final being held in Pamekasan in September. The bulls are specially fed on beer, eggs and chillies, which may account for their 30mph speeds over the 100 metre course!

Though there are many people throughout this vast country only just managing to get by, feast days and festivals, where food plays an important and vital part, abound. Along all the roads in Bali are little temples, where daily offerings of fruit and flowers are made to the gods. The Balinese have an inner faith and grace that seems to transcend the trappings of tourism. It is rare to meet anyone who has been there who would not like to return to this Garden of Eden.

Eating out is easy in the warm tropical climate. People seem to eat all the time! Padang restaurants are popular, with a vast choice of dishes to choose from. We were always very impressed by the waiters, who carry up to ten different plates of food to your table, balanced cleverly on their arms. In Padang restaurants, you help yourself, then the plates are cleared away and you only pay for what you have eaten!

A buffet-style meal makes sense when serving Indonesian food. Guests put a few spoonfuls of rice in wide-brimmed soup plates, moisten them

At an early morning market at Nusa Penida, on the island of Bali, shoppers are buying small, silvery fish on bamboo skewers, ready for the barbecue.

with one of the soups, usually a *sayur*, and then put spoonfuls of whatever they fancy from the dishes on offer individually round the edge of the plate. The dish is topped with perhaps a few crisp deep-fried onions, a spot of chilli sambal and a crisp prawn cracker, to complete the full range of textures and flavours that make up a truly memorable Indonesian meal.

For a lavish spread for 8–10 people, the following would be a suitable selection of dishes:

Vegetable Broth with Minced Beef
Rendang
Spicy Squid
Festive Rice
Sweetcorn Fritters
Fruit and Vegetable Salad with
Sweet and Sour Dressing
Steamed Coconut Custard

This would be eaten with a spoon and fork. Usually soft drinks or beer are served with the meal.

Selemat makan "Good eating", as they say in Indonesia.

INGREDIENTS

BANANA LEAVES

Banana leaves are used as the South-east Asian answer to kitchen foil and are available from many oriental supermarkets in the UK. Make the leaves more pliable by plunging them into boiling water or holding them over a flame, before placing the ingredients for cooking inside. Make into a neat parcel and secure with a saté stick or a fine skewer. Food wrapped in this way is sometimes steamed and frequently grilled and gains flavour from the banana leaf itself.

BANGKUANG (YAMBEAN)

These are the same shape as a turnip but with a smooth, light golden skin, which should be peeled thinly. The texture is somewhere between an apple and a hard pear. Peel and cut in julienne strips, to use in stir-fries, spring rolls or salads.

BEAN CURD

These fragile looking 7.5cm/3in cubes are available fresh. They are made from soya bean milk set with gypsum and are popular with vegetarians. In spite of its bland flavour, bean curd is full of protein. It will keep in the fridge for 3–4 days, if covered with fresh water daily. A long-life version is available; once it is opened, use it as fresh and store the bean curd as directed on the pack.

Clockwise from left: black rice, bean thread cellophane noodles and dried egg noodles.

Clockwise from top: large purple aubergines, garden eggs and small yellow aubergines.

To use bean curd from the freezer, pour boiling water over it in a bowl. Drain and squeeze; use whole or slice.

Tempe is made from whole fermented soya beans, to give a cake which is bursting with protein, plus iron and vitamin B. Cut into cubes or slices and add to dishes as directed on the packet.

BEANSPROUTS

Readily available from greengrocers and supermarkets. Chill in the packet and use as soon as possible. Most sprouted beans come from mung beans, though soya beans are also available. Both can be sprouted at home.

CHILLIES

Available from greengrocers and supermarkets, the chilli is grown on a dwarf bush with small dense green leaves, white flowers and red or green finger shaped fruit. In general, the green chilli is less hot and has a rather earthy heat; the red is usually hotter and is sometimes very fiery.

To prepare, remove the cap from the stalk end and slit it from top to bottom with a small knife. Under running water, scoop out the seeds (unless you like food fiercely hot) with the knife point. Use rubber gloves or wash your hands thoroughly with soap and water.

Use the recipe for Chilli Sambal, if you have a plentiful supply of chillies, or buy the jars of chopped chilli available from large supermarkets. After opening, keep in the fridge.

COCONUT MILK AND CREAM

In South-east Asia, the canned variety is often used, simply for convenience. (The liquid inside a whole coconut is coconut juice and not coconut milk – it makes a refreshing drink when chilled.) Once opened, chill canned milk for 4–5 days or freeze it.

Coconut cream is available in 200ml/7fl oz cartons and a carton is the equivalent of one coconut.

Instant powdered coconut milk is widely available. Slabs of frozen coconut milk are available too.

Desiccated coconut is a very successful way of obtaining good-quality coconut milk and cream. Buy unsweetened coconut; larger and cheaper quantities can be bought in oriental supermarkets. Empty 225g/8oz/4 cups into a food processor with 475ml/16fl oz/2 cups boiling water. Process for 20–30 seconds and leave to cool. If making several batches, empty each lot into a large bowl after processing and allow to cool. Place a large sieve over a large bowl and line it with muslin. Ladle some of the cooled mixture into the muslin, fold the edges

Clockwise from left: Coconut shells with the meat removed, whole fresh coconut and coconut cream.

Clockwise from left: fresh root ginger, fresh galangal roots and fresh turmeric roots, cut to show their vivid colour.

over the coconut and twist the ends, to squeeze out the maximum amount of milk. Repeat with the remaining coconut. You can use the squeezed coconut to make a second batch, but it will not be nearly as rich.

CORIANDER
Available all over South-east Asia, the seeds are more often used than the leaves in Indonesian cuisine. The flavour is greatly enhanced by dry-frying.

DUAN SALAM LEAVES
Only available dried, these resemble bay leaves, which are a good substitute if duan salam leaves are hard to find.

GINGER
Fresh root ginger has a silvery brown skin that can be scraped or peeled. Slice and either chop or pound the flesh, and use as soon as possible for maximum flavour. Bruised ginger is suggested in some recipes: give it a sharp blow with the end of a rolling pin or use a pestle and mortar. Store in the fridge vegetable box, wrapped in kitchen paper. Chopped ginger is available in jars and keeps well in the fridge.

LEMON GRASS
An essential ingredient in the cooking of South-east Asia, lemon grass has a magical aroma and flavour. Fresh stems

are easy to come by in supermarkets, oriental stores and good greengrocers. To prepare for a spice paste, for instance, discard the root end and then cut the lower 6cm/2¹/₂in and smell the citrus aroma as you do this. Slice the lower, bulbous piece and grind it as directed, then bruise the top half and add it to the curry to infuse its flavour or use it as a brush with which to anoint the meat on saté sticks. Wrap closely in kitchen paper or newspaper and store in the vegetable box in the fridge. Fresh, ground lemon grass is available in jars.

LENGKUAS (laos, greater galangal)
A member of the ginger family, which is used more than ginger in Indonesian cooking. The root is creamy coloured, with rings on the skin, and may have pink nodules rather like very young ginger.

To prepare, trim off the size of piece indicated in the recipe. Trim off any knobbly bits, then peel carefully as the skin has an unpleasant taste and is tough. Slice to use in a paste and use up as soon as possible after peeling, to preserve the flavour. The flesh is much more woody and fibrous than ginger and has a distinctive, pine-like smell. Wrap in kitchen paper or newspaper and store in the vegetable box in the fridge. Dried lengkuas powder can be bought; use 5ml/1 tsp to replace each 2.5cm/1in of fresh lengkuas. It cannot match the fresh for flavour.

From left: fresh coriander root and leaves, lemon grass and lime leaves.

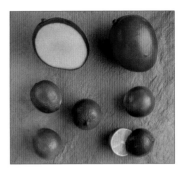

Clockwise from top left: mango cut in half, whole mango, halved lime and whole limes.

LIME LEAVES (duan jeruk)
These glossy, dark green leaves come from the kaffir lime tree. They have a pleasing, distinctive smell and can be torn or left whole. Leaves can be frozen and used from the freezer.

MACADAMIA NUTS (kemiri, buah keras and candlenuts)
Popular as a cocktail snack here and an essential ingredient in Indonesian cooking. Marble-sized nuts which, when ground, act as a thickening agent in many recipes. For convenience, almonds are given as an alternative, but do try to find the macadamia or even Brazil nuts, if possible.

NOODLES (mee/mie)
Add dried egg noodles to a large pan of boiling, salted water and cook for 3–5 minutes. Stir to prevent the noodles from settling on the base of the pan. Drain and rinse with cold water, to wash out starch and prevent the noodles from sticking together.

Fresh egg noodles take only 1 minute to cook in salted, fast-boiling water. Drain as above and then use as directed.

Rice noodles (rice sticks) can be soaked ahead of cooking, either in cold water for some time or in warm water for just a few minutes. Plunge into fast-boiling, salted water. Allow to return to the boil and then remove from the

From left: fresh red chillies, pandan leaves, dried red chillies and dried green chillies.

heat and leave for 2 minutes only, till just cooked. Test one piece and then drain and rinse well with cold water, if not to be used immediately.

Bean thread cellophane noodles (*su-un*) are made from mung-bean flour and gathered into a skein. Soak in cold water, cut into lengths with scissors and place in boiling water for 1 minute. Drain and use as required.

PANDAN LEAVES (screwpine)

Leaves like a gladioli in size and shape, which impart a warm aroma when cooked. Available fresh, in bunches, pandan leaves are used to flavour rice and desserts. Pull the tines of a fork through a leaf to tear it and release the flavour, and tie the leaf in a knot so that it is easy to extricate.

RICE

We are more discerning these days about the rice we eat. Without doubt Thai fragrant rice rightly holds its high reputation for quality and fragrance. Many homes have a rice cooker but if not, use the following method for boiled rice.

Boiled rice: wash 225g/8oz/1¼ cups

Clockwise from top left: dried whole mushrooms, red-skinned peanuts in their shells, purple-skinned shallots, tamarind with part of the pod removed and whole tamarind pods.

of rice in several changes of water, until the water looks clear. Place in a pan, with 500ml/18fl oz/2¼ cups of water and bring to the boil. Reduce the heat, stir, cover the pan and cook gently for 12–15 minutes. Stir with a chopstick or roasting fork, so as not to break up the grains. Cover and leave for 3–4 minutes before using; or wrap the pan in a blanket to keep the rice warm for at least 1–1½ hours.

SOY SAUCE

Soy sauce is made from fermented soya beans, wheat grain, salt and water. There are two main varieties: thick, sometimes referred to as black, and thin, curiously referred to as white! In Indonesia, it is called *kecap asin*. *Kecap sedang* is of medium consistency but in Indonesia, ordinary soy sauce, called *kecap manis*, is preferred, because it is thicker and sweeter.

TAMARIND (asam jawa)

Tamarind is used to add tartness to recipes, just as we might use vinegar or lemon juice. A convenient tamarind concentrate is available.

The pulp is sold in a block. In the recipes, 5ml/1 tsp tamarind pulp is mixed with warm water. Soak, then mix with your fingers, to release the pulp from the seeds. Strain and discard the pulp and seeds. Use as directed. Jars of ready-made juice are available.

TERASI (blachan, balachan)

An essential ingredient, common to the countries of South-east Asia, made from fermented shrimps or prawns, with salt, pounded into a paste and sold in blocks. Wrap a cube in a foil parcel and place in a dry frying pan over a gentle heat for 5 minutes, turning from time to time. This takes away the rawness from the terasi and also avoids filling the kitchen with the strong and distinctive smell. If the terasi is to be fried in the recipe, this preliminary cooking can be omitted.

TURMERIC

Turmeric is a member of the ginger family. When peeled or scraped, a rich golden root is revealed. It gives a superb colour to sauces or rice, as well as a good flavour and a warm aroma. Wear rubber gloves to prevent staining.

EQUIPMENT IN THE KITCHEN

Left: Wok with non-stick surface and closely-fitting lid and wooden spatula. The wok can double as a steamer, or food can be kept warm on the rack.

WOK

In Indonesia, the wok is called a *wajan*. There are many different qualities of wok on sale and the best advice is to go for the heaviest quality you can find; thin, lightweight woks are always a disappointment, because you are very likely to burn the food, which is invariably cooked at a high temperature. The wok is ideal, not only for stir-frying, but for deep-frying too. If you have a gas cooker, choose one with a metal stand, on which the wok sits firmly and safely during cooking. There are several types of electric woks on sale, frequently with non-stick surfaces, so you must use wooden or plastic tools with these.

One useful cooking tip is to warm the wok gently before adding the oil for cooking. The oil then floods easily over the surface of the warm pan and prevents food from sticking. The amount of oil needed in a wok is considerably less than required in a conventional pan, which is a real plus-point in these health-conscious days.

FOOD PROCESSOR OR PESTLE AND MORTAR

Both feature countless times in this book in the preparation of spice pastes and the blending of ingredients. When time is short a food processor is invaluable; it is the next-best thing to a helper in the kitchen. The various blade attachments are useful when thin, even slices of onion, cucumber and so on are required. When preparing spice pastes, fibrous ingredients, such as ginger, lengkuas and lemon grass, are best sliced thinly before processing, to obtain a smoother paste. Alternatively, bruise with the pestle and in the mortar first. Some oil can be added to the spice paste ingredients, to ease the blending, but remember to reduce the amount for frying the paste.

A deep granite pestle and mortar, sold in many oriental superstores and markets, which is pitted inside, is ideal for finely pounding the wet spices that are such an important part of the preparation of the spice paste. This may seem laborious to us, in our instant world, but to oriental cooks this is a gratifying and pleasurable activity.

A small coffee grinder is useful where small quantities of dry spices are to be pounded, but it is advisable to keep it exclusively for this purpose.

STEAMERS

Bamboo, stacking-type steamers are available in a host of sizes from a wide range of stores. When not in use, they look very attractive on a shelf in the kitchen. Like almost all utensils in the oriental kitchen, they are multi-purpose. Indeed the baskets can be used for serving as well as cooking the foods. Where small items are being cooked, line the baskets with a piece of rinsed muslin. Several baskets can be stacked one on top of the other, with the lid set on top. These are then placed over the wok and the boiling water replenished as required. For cooking large items, such as a whole fish in a dish, place in the wok over

water, cover with a lid and keep an eye on the water level while the food is steaming.

BARBECUE

In Indonesia they often use a special barbecue unit for cooking *satés*, which is very lightweight and requires very little charcoal. A gas or electric grill can be used, of course, but food that has been cooked over charcoal has an extra special flavour. In Indonesia, a fan made from woven palm fronds is used to keep the charcoal glowing. Again, this looks very attractive hanging up in the kitchen, when not in use.

RICE COOKER

These are immensely popular in Indonesia and you can see why, when up to three meals a day can be rice-based. The great advantage of the rice cooker is that it is foolproof, producing perfect rice every time, and will happily keep the rice warm for up to five hours. Leftover rice can be reheated the following day and the cooker may also be used for steaming many other dishes.

Above: Attractive two-tiered bamboo steamer with lid, useful for meat or fish and vegetable dishes which are to be steamed together.

SOUPS AND SNACKS

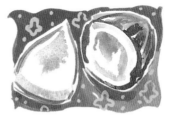

All round the clock, in cities, towns and large villages, warungs *or street vendors provide nourishing snack food at a moment's notice. The* kroepoek *(prawn cracker) seller has two huge containers, like large dustbins, suspended at either end of a bamboo pole and moves along at a cracking pace. Satés are a firm favourite; these delicious morsels of beef, prawn, pork or lamb on bamboo skewers, served with either a peanut or soy-based sauce, need no introduction. Soup is not served as a separate course but used to moisten a bowl of rice, with other dishes and accompaniments ranged around it.* Soto *is a main-course soup;* sop *is a clear soup with meat, chicken and some vegetables.* Sayur *is a vegetable soup, often made with a coconut-flavoured stock.*

Spicy Meat Patties with Coconut

Spicy meat patties, known as *Rempah*, with a hint of coconut, often feature as one of the delicious accompaniments in an Indonesian-style buffet.

INGREDIENTS

Makes 22

115g/4oz freshly grated coconut, or desiccated coconut, soaked in 60–90ml/4–6 tbsp boiling water
350g/12oz finely minced beef
2.5ml/½ tsp each coriander and cumin seeds, dry-fried
1 garlic clove, crushed
a little beaten egg
15–30ml/1–2 tbsp plain flour
groundnut oil for frying
salt
thin lemon or lime wedges, to serve

1 Mix the moistened coconut with the minced beef.

2 Grind the dry-fried coriander and cumin seeds with a pestle and mortar. Add the ground spices to the meat and coconut mixture together with the garlic, salt to taste, and sufficient beaten egg to bind.

3 Divide the meat into evenly sized portions, the size of a walnut, and form into patty shapes.

4 Dust with flour. Heat the oil and then fry the patties for 4–5 minutes until both sides are golden brown and cooked through. Serve with lemon or lime wedges, to squeeze over.

Sweetcorn Fritters

There is no doubt that freshly cooked sweetcorn is best for this recipe, called *Perkedel Jagung*. Do not add salt to the water, because this toughens the outer husk.

INGREDIENTS

Makes 20

2 fresh corn on the cob, or 350g/12oz can sweetcorn kernels
2 macadamia nuts or 4 almonds
1 garlic clove
1 onion, quartered
1cm/½in fresh *lengkuas*, peeled and sliced
5ml/1 tsp ground coriander
30–45ml/2–3 tbsp oil
3 eggs, beaten
30ml/2 tbsp desiccated coconut
2 spring onions, finely shredded
a few celery leaves, finely shredded (optional)
salt

1 Cook the corn on the cob in boiling water for 7–8 minutes. Drain, cool slightly and, using a sharp knife, strip the kernels from the cob. If using canned sweetcorn, drain well.

2 Grind the nuts, garlic, onion, *lengkuas* and coriander to a fine paste in a food processor or pestle and mortar. Heat a little oil and fry the paste until it gives off a spicy aroma.

3 Add the fried spices to the beaten eggs with the coconut, spring onions and celery leaves, if using. Add salt to taste with the corn kernels.

4 Heat the remaining oil in a shallow frying pan. Drop large spoonfuls of batter into the pan and cook for 2–3 minutes until golden. Flip the fritters over with a fish slice and cook until golden brown and crispy. Only cook three or four fritters at a time.

Clear Soup with Meatballs

INGREDIENTS

Serves 8
For the meatballs
175g/6oz very finely minced beef
1 small onion, very finely chopped
1–2 garlic cloves, crushed
15ml/1 tbsp cornflour
a little egg white, lightly beaten
salt and freshly ground black pepper

For the soup
4–6 Chinese mushrooms, soaked in
    warm water for 30 minutes
30ml/2 tbsp groundnut oil
1 large onion, finely chopped
2 garlic cloves, finely crushed
1cm/½ in fresh root ginger, bruised
2 litres/3½ pints/8 cups beef or
    chicken stock, including soaking
    liquid from the mushrooms
30ml/2 tbsp soy sauce
115g/4oz curly kale, spinach or
    Chinese leaves, shredded

1 First prepare the meatballs. Mix
the beef with the onion, garlic,
cornflour and seasoning in a food
processor and then bind with sufficient
egg white to make a firm mixture.
With wetted hands, roll into tiny, bite-
size balls and set aside.

2 Drain the mushrooms and reserve
the soaking liquid to add to the
stock. Trim off and discard the stalks.
Slice the caps finely and set aside.

3 Heat a wok or large saucepan and
add the oil. Fry the onion, garlic
and ginger to bring out the flavour, but
do not allow to brown.

4 When the onion is soft, pour in
the stock. Bring to the boil, then
stir in the soy sauce and mushroom
slices and simmer for 10 minutes. Add
the meatballs and cook for 10 minutes.

5 Just before serving, remove the
ginger. Stir in the shredded curly
kale, spinach or Chinese leaves. Heat
through for 1 minute only: no longer
or the leaves will be overcooked. Serve
the soup immediately.

Tamarind Soup with Peanuts and Vegetables

ayur Asam is a colourful and
efreshing soup from Jakarta with
nore than a hint of sharpness.

NGREDIENTS

erves 4 or 8 as part of a buffet
or the spice paste
shallots or 1 medium red
onion, sliced
garlic cloves, crushed
.5cm/1in *lengkuas*, peeled and sliced
–2 fresh red chillies, seeded and sliced
5g/1oz raw peanuts
cm/½in cube *terasi*, prepared
.2 litres/2 pints/5 cups well-
flavoured stock
0–75g/2–3oz salted peanuts,
lightly crushed
5–30ml/1–2 tbsp dark brown sugar
ml/1 tsp tamarind pulp, soaked in
75ml/5 tbsp warm water for
15 minutes
alt

or the vegetables
chayote, thinly peeled, seeds
removed, flesh finely sliced
15g/4oz French beans, trimmed and
finely sliced
0g/2oz sweetcorn kernels (optional)
andful green leaves, such as
watercress, rocket or Chinese leaves,
finely shredded
fresh green chilli, sliced, to garnish

1 Prepare the spice paste by grinding
the shallots or onion, garlic,
ngkuas, chillies, raw peanuts and *terasi*
o a paste in a food processor or with a
estle and mortar.

2 Pour in some of the stock to
moisten and then pour this mixture
into a pan or wok, adding the rest of
the stock. Cook for 15 minutes with
the lightly crushed peanuts and sugar.

3 Strain the tamarind, discarding the
seeds, and reserve the juice.

4 About 5 minutes before serving,
add the chayote slices, beans and
sweetcorn, if using, to the soup and
cook fairly rapidly. At the last minute,
add the green leaves and salt to taste.

5 Add the tamarind juice and taste
for seasoning. Serve, garnished
with slices of green chilli.

Vegetable Broth with Minced Beef

INGREDIENTS

Serves 6

30ml/2 tbsp groundnut oil
115g/4oz finely minced beef
1 large onion, grated or finely chopped
1 garlic clove, crushed
1–2 fresh chillies, seeded and chopped
1cm/½in cube *terasi*, prepared
3 macadamia nuts or 6 almonds,
   finely ground
1 carrot, finely grated
5ml/1 tsp brown sugar
1 litre/1¾ pints/4 cups chicken stock
50g/2oz dried shrimps, soaked in warm
   water for 10 minutes
225g/8oz spinach, rinsed and
   finely shredded
8 baby sweetcorn, sliced, or 200g/7oz
   canned sweetcorn kernels
1 large tomato, chopped
juice of ½ lemon
salt

1 Heat the oil in a saucepan. Add the beef, onion and garlic and cook, stirring, until the meat changes colour.

2 Add the chillies, *terasi*, nuts, carrot, sugar and salt to taste.

3 Add the stock and bring gently to the boil. Reduce the heat to a simmer and then add the soaked shrimps, with their soaking liquid. Simmer for about 10 minutes.

4 A few minutes before serving, add the spinach, sweetcorn, tomato and lemon juice. Simmer for a minute or two, to heat through. Do not overcool at this stage because this will spoil the appearance and the taste of the *sayur*.

--- COOK'S TIP ---

To make this broth, *Sayur Menir,* very hot and spicy, add the seeds from the chillies.

Omelettes with Spicy Meat Filling

INGREDIENTS

Serves 4

For the filling

1cm/½in cube *terasi*
3 garlic cloves, crushed
4 macadamia nuts or 8 almonds
1cm/½in fresh *lengkuas*, peeled and
   sliced, or 5ml/1 tsp *lengkuas*
   powder (optional)
5ml/1 tsp ground coriander
2.5ml/½ tsp ground turmeric
5ml/1 tsp salt
30ml/2 tbsp oil
225g/8oz minced beef
2 spring onions, chopped
½ celery stick, finely chopped
30–45ml/2–3 tbsp coconut milk

For the omelettes

oil for frying
4 eggs, beaten with 60ml/4 tbsp water
salt and freshly ground black pepper
salad and celery leaves, to serve

1 Grind the *terasi* to a paste, in a food processor or with a pestle and mortar, with the garlic, nuts and fresh *lengkuas*, if using. Add the coriander, turmeric, *lengkuas* powder, (if using), and the salt.

2 Heat the oil and fry the mixture for 1–2 minutes. Stir in the beef and cook until it changes colour. Continue to cook for 2–3 minutes. Stir in the spring onions, celery and coconut milk. Cover and cook gently for 5 minutes.

3 Meanwhile, prepare the omelettes. Heat a little oil in an omelette or frying pan. Season the eggs and use to make four thin omelettes in the usual way. When each omelette is almost cooked, spoon a quarter of the filling on top and roll up. Keep warm while making the remaining omelettes.

4 Cut the rolled omelettes in half and arrange on a serving dish. Serve garnished with a few salad and celery leaves.

Spicy Meat-filled Parcels

In Indonesia the finest gossamer dough is made for *Martabak*. You can achieve equally good results using ready-made filo pastry or spring roll wrappers.

INGREDIENTS

Makes 16

450g/1lb lean minced beef
2 small onions, finely chopped
2 small leeks, very
   finely chopped
2 garlic cloves, crushed
10ml/2 tsp coriander seeds, dry-fried
   and ground
5ml/1 tsp cumin seeds, dry-fried
   and ground
5–10ml/1–2 tsp mild curry powder
2 eggs, beaten
400g/14oz packet filo pastry
45–60ml/3–4 tbsp sunflower oil
salt and freshly ground black pepper
light soy sauce, to serve

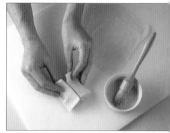

1 To make the filling, mix the meat with the onions, leeks, garlic, coriander, cumin, curry powder and seasoning. Turn into a heated wok, without oil, and stir all the time, until the meat has changed colour and looks cooked, about 5 minutes.

2 Allow to cool and then mix in enough beaten egg to bind to a soft consistency. Any leftover egg can be used to seal the edges of the dough; otherwise, use milk.

3 Brush a sheet of filo with oil and lay another sheet on top. Cut the sheets in half. Place a large spoonful of the filling on each double piece of filo. Fold the sides to the middle so that the edges just overlap. Brush these edges with either beaten egg or milk and fold the other two sides to the middle in the same way, so that you now have a square parcel shape. Make sure that the parcel is as flat as possible, to speed cooking. Repeat with the remaining fifteen parcels and place on a floured tray in the fridge.

4 Heat the remaining oil in a shallow pan and cook several parcels at a time, depending on the size of the pan. Cook for 3 minutes on the first side and then turn them over and cook for a further 2 minutes, or until heated through. Cook the remaining parcels in the same way and serve hot, sprinkled with light soy sauce.

5 If preferred, these spicy parcels can be cooked in a hot oven at 200°C/400°F/Gas 6 for 20 minutes. Glaze with more beaten egg before baking for a rich, golden colour.

Pork Satés

Though Indonesia is a Muslim country there have been waves of Chinese immigrants, who have made an enormous contribution to the richness of its cuisine, including the introduction of pork in many recipes. Beef or lamb could be used for *Saté Babi Ketjap* instead.

INGREDIENTS

Makes 12–16 skewers
500g/1¼lb pork fillet

For the marinade
150ml/¼ pint/⅔ cup dark soy sauce
3–4 garlic cloves, crushed
45ml/3 tbsp groundnut oil
50g/2oz peanuts, finely
    crushed (optional)
salt and freshly ground pepper

For the sauce
1 onion, finely chopped
2–3 fresh red chillies, seeded and
    ground, or 15ml/1 tbsp Chilli Sambal
75ml/3fl oz/⅓ cup dark soy sauce
60–90ml/4–6 tbsp water
juice of 1–2 limes or 1 large lemon
50g/2oz peanuts, coarsely ground

To serve
lime wedges
Deep-fried Onions

1 Wipe and trim the meat. Cut the pork into 2.5cm/1in cubes or into thin strips about 1cm/½in wide by 5cm/2in long.

2 Blend the dark soy sauce, garlic and oil together with seasoning and the crushed peanuts, if using. Pour over the meat and allow to marinate for at least 1 hour, turning in the marinade from time to time.

3 If using wooden or bamboo skewers, soak them in water for 1 hour so that they don't burn when the *satés* are being cooked. Then thread three or four pieces of meat on to one end of each of the skewers.

4 Make the sauce. Put the onion, chillies or Chilli Sambal, soy sauce and water in a saucepan. Bring to the boil, and simmer gently for 4–5 minutes. Cool, then stir in the lime or lemon juice. Add the coarsely ground peanuts to the sauce just before serving. Preheat the grill or barbecue.

5 Cook the *satés*, turning frequently, until tender, about 5–8 minutes. Garnish with lime wedges and Deep-fried Onions and serve with the sauce.

Peanut Fritters

You can buy rice powder and rice flour in any Asian shop. For this recipe, *Rempeyak Kacang*, it is best to use the rice flour, which is ideal as it has a slightly more grainy texture. Peanut fritters are easy and quick to prepare. They go well with Festive Rice and make a good addition to a buffet.

INGREDIENTS

Makes 15–20
50g/2oz rice flour
2.5ml/½ tsp baking powder
1 garlic clove, crushed
2.5ml/½ tsp ground coriander
2 pinches ground cumin
2.5ml/½ tsp ground turmeric
50g/2oz peanuts, lightly crushed
about 150ml/¼ pint/⅔ cup water, or
  coconut milk or a mixture of both
oil for shallow-frying
salt
coriander leaves, to garnish

1 Put the rice flour, salt to taste and baking powder into a bowl. Add the garlic, coriander, cumin, turmeric and peanuts. Gradually stir in the water or coconut milk, to make a smooth, slightly runny batter.

2 Heat a little oil in a frying pan. Use a dessertspoon to spoon the batter into the pan and cook several fritters at a time. When the tops are no longer runny and the undersides are lacy and golden brown, turn them over with a spatula and cook the other sides until crisp and brown.

3 Lift out and drain on kitchen paper. Either use immediately or cool and store in an airtight tin.

4 To reheat the fritters, arrange in a single layer on a large baking sheet. Bake at 180°C/350°F/Gas 4 for about 10 minutes. Garnish with coriander.

—— Cook's Tip ——

You can use either salted or unsalted peanuts in this recipe, but remember to adjust the seasoning accordingly.

Prawn Crackers

In Indonesia one can find a wide range of *kroepoek* (the 'oe' spelling betrays the Dutch influence). They can be made from rice, wheat, corn or cassava and so have differing flavours – rather like our crisps. You may use the tiny Chinese-style prawn crackers which are more readily available from oriental stores and some large supermarkets.

INGREDIENTS

oil for deep-frying
225g/8oz packet prawn crackers, or
½ x 500g/1¼lb packet large
  Indonesian prawn crackers

1 Heat the oil in a deep-frying pan to 190°C/375°F, or when a cube of day-old bread browns in 30 seconds.

2 Fry just one of the large *kroepoek* at a time, especially if they are being cooked whole. Cook 8–10 small crackers at a time.

3 As soon as they have expanded and become very puffy, remove them immediately from the oil with a slotted spoon. Do not allow them to colour. Drain the crackers on kitchen paper. They can be cooked a few hours in advance and any leftovers can be kept in an airtight container.

Lamb Satés

INGREDIENTS

Makes 25–30 skewers

1kg/2¼lb leg of lamb, boned
3 garlic cloves, crushed
15–30ml/1–2 tbsp Chilli Sambal or
  3–4 fresh chillies, seeded and ground,
  or 5–10ml/1–2 tsp chilli powder
60–90ml/4–6 tbsp dark soy sauce
juice of 1 lemon
salt and freshly ground black pepper
oil for brushing

For the sauce

6 garlic cloves, crushed
15ml/1 tbsp Chilli Sambal or 2–3 fresh
  chillies, seeded and ground
90ml/6 tbsp dark soy sauce
25ml/1½ tbsp lemon juice
30ml/2 tbsp boiling water

To serve

small onion pieces
cucumber wedges
Compressed-rice Shapes (optional)

1 Cut the lamb into thick slices and then into neat 1cm/½in cubes. Remove any pieces of gristle but do not trim off any of the fat because this keeps the *satés* moist during cooking and enhances the flavour.

> ——— VARIATION ———
>
> Lamb neck fillet is now widely available in supermarkets and can be used instead of boned leg. Brush the lamb fillet with oil before grilling.

2 Blend the garlic, Chilli Sambal, ground fresh chillies or chilli powder, soy sauce, lemon juice and seasoning to a paste in a food processor or with a pestle and mortar. Pour over the lamb. Cover and leave in a cool place for at least an hour. Soak wooden or bamboo skewers in water so that they won't burn during cooking.

3 Prepare the sauce. Put the garlic cloves into a bowl. Add the Chilli Sambal or chillies, soy sauce, lemon juice and boiling water. Stir well.

4 Thread the meat on to the skewers. Brush with oil and cook under the grill, turning often. Brush each *saté* with a little of the sauce and serve hot, with small pieces of onion, cucumber and the rice shapes, if using. Serve with the remaining sauce.

Prawn Satés

For *Saté Udang*, king prawns look spectacular and taste wonderful. The spicy coconut marinade marries beautifully with the prawns and is also excellent when used with firm cubes of monkfish or halibut and cooked in the same way.

INGREDIENTS

Makes 4 skewers
12 uncooked king prawns

For the marinade

5mm/¼in cube *terasi*
1 garlic clove, crushed
1 lemon grass stem, lower 6cm/2½in sliced, top reserved
3–4 macadamia nuts or 6–8 almonds
2.5ml/½ tsp chilli powder
salt
oil for frying
120ml/4fl oz/½ cup coconut milk
2.5ml/½ tsp tamarind pulp, soaked in 30ml/2 tbsp water, then strained and juice reserved

To serve

Peanut Sauce
Compressed-rice Shapes (optional)
cucumber cubes (optional)
lemon wedges

1 Remove the heads from the prawns. Peel the prawns and remove the spinal cord, if liked. Using a small sharp knife, make an incision along the underbody of each prawn, without cutting it completely in half and open it up like a book. Thread 3 of the prawns on to each skewer.

2 Make the marinade. Grind the *terasi*, garlic, lemon grass slices, nuts, chilli powder and a little salt to a paste in a food processor or with a pestle and mortar.

3 Fry the paste in oil, for 1 minute. Add the coconut milk and tamarind juice. Simmer for 1 minute. Cool. Pour over the prawns and leave for 1 hour.

4 Cook the prawns under a hot grill or on the barbecue for 3 minutes or until cooked through. Beat the top part of the lemon grass with the end of a rolling pin, to make it into a brush. Use this to brush the prawns with the marinade during cooking.

5 Serve on a platter, with the Peanut Sauce, rice shapes and cucumber cubes, if using, and lemon wedges.

Spiced Vegetable Soup with Chicken and Prawns

INGREDIENTS

Serves 6–8

1 onion, ½ cut in two, ½ sliced
2 garlic cloves, crushed
1 fresh red or green chilli, seeded
 and sliced
1cm/½in cube *terasi*
3 macadamia nuts or 6 almonds
1cm/½in *lengkuas*, peeled and sliced, or
 5ml/1 tsp *lengkuas* powder
5ml/1 tsp sugar
oil for frying
225g/8oz boned, skinned chicken
 breast, cut in 1cm/½in cubes
300ml/½ pint/1¼ cups coconut milk
1.2 litres/2 pints/5 cups chicken stock
1 aubergine, diced
225g/8oz French beans, chopped
small wedge of crisp white
 cabbage, shredded
1 red pepper, seeded and finely sliced
115g/4oz cooked, peeled prawns
salt and freshly ground black pepper

1 Grind the onion quarters, garlic, chilli, *terasi*, nuts, *lengkuas* and sugar to a paste in a food processor or with a pestle and mortar.

2 Heat a wok, add the oil and then fry the paste, without browning, until it gives off a rich aroma. Add the sliced onion and chicken cubes and cook for 3–4 minutes. Stir in the coconut milk and stock. Bring to the boil and simmer for a few minutes.

3 Add the diced aubergine to the soup, with the beans, and cook for only a few minutes, until the beans are almost cooked.

4 A few minutes before serving, stir the cabbage, red pepper and prawns into the soup. The vegetables should be cooked so that they are still crunchy and the prawns merely heated through. Taste the soup and adjust the seasoning if necessary.

Spiced Beef Satés

INGREDIENTS

Makes 18 skewers

450g/1lb rump steak, cut in 1cm/½in
 slices or strips
5ml/1 tsp coriander seeds, dry-fried
 and ground
2.5ml/½ tsp cumin seeds, dry-fried
 and ground
5ml/1 tsp tamarind pulp
1 small onion
2 garlic cloves
15ml/1 tbsp brown sugar
15ml/1 tbsp dark soy sauce
salt

To serve
cucumber chunks
lemon or lime wedges
Sambal Kecap

1 Mix the meat and spices in a non-metallic bowl. Soak the tamarind pulp in 75ml/3fl oz/⅓ cup water.

2 Strain the tamarind and reserve the juice. Put the onion, garlic, tamarind juice, sugar and soy sauce in a food processor and blend well. Alternatively, pound the onion and garlic in a mortar with a pestle, and add the remaining ingredients.

3 Pour the marinade over the meat and spices in the bowl and toss well together. Leave for at least 1 hour. Meanwhile, soak some bamboo skewers in water to prevent them from burning whilst cooking.

4 Preheat the grill. Thread 5 or 6 pieces of meat on to each of the skewers and sprinkle the meat with salt. Place under the hot grill or, even better, over a charcoal barbecue, and cook, turning frequently, until tender. Baste with the marinade throughout the cooking, turning the skewers over from time to time.

5 Serve on a platter garnished with cucumber chunks and wedges of lemon or lime to squeeze over the *satés*. Put the Sambal Kecap in a small bowl and serve alongside.

Deep-fried Wonton Cushions with Sambal Kecap

Pangsit Goreng are popular as party fare or for a quick snack.

INGREDIENTS

Makes 40

115g/4oz pork fillet, trimmed
   and sliced
225g/8oz cooked, peeled prawns
2–3 garlic cloves, crushed
2 spring onions, roughly chopped
15ml/1 tbsp cornflour
about 40 wonton wrappers
oil for deep-frying
salt and freshly ground black pepper

For the Sambal Kecap

1–2 fresh red chillies, seeded and sliced
1–2 garlic cloves, crushed
45ml/3 tbsp dark soy sauce
45–60ml/3–4 tbsp lemon or lime juice
15–30ml/1–2 tbsp water

1 Grind the slices of pork finely in a food processor. Add the prawns, garlic, spring onions and cornflour. Season to taste and then process briefly.

2 Place a little of the prepared filling on to each wonton wrapper, just off centre, with the skin shaped like a diamond in front of you. Dampen all the edges, except for the uppermost corner of the diamond.

3 Lift the corner nearest to you towards the filling and then roll up the wrapper once more, to cover the filling. Turn over. Bring the two extreme corners together, sealing one on top of the other. Squeeze lightly, to plump up the filling. Repeat until all the wrappers and the filling are used up. The prepared "cushions" can be frozen at this stage. Any leftover wonton wrappers can be wrapped and stored in the freezer as well.

4 Meanwhile, prepare the Sambal. Mix the chillies and garlic together and then stir in the dark soy sauce, lemon or lime juice and water. Pour into a serving bowl and set aside.

5 Heat the oil in a deep-frying pan to 190°C/375°F, or when a cube of day-old bread browns in 30 seconds. Deep-fry the wonton cushions, a few at a time, for about 2–3 minutes, or until cooked through, crisp and golden brown. Remove the wontons with a slotted spoon and drain on kitchen paper. If cooking from frozen, allow 4 minutes. Serve on a large platter together with the Sambal Kecap.

Balinese Vegetable Soup

ny seasonal vegetables can be
sed in *Sayur Oelih*.

NGREDIENTS

erves 8

25g/8oz green beans
2 litres/2 pints/5 cups boiling water
00ml/14fl oz/1²/₃ cups coconut milk
garlic clove
macadamia nuts or 4 almonds
cm/¹/₂ in cube *terasi*
0–15ml/2–3 tsp coriander seeds, dry-
fried and ground
il for frying
onion, finely sliced
duan salam or bay leaves
25g/8oz beansprouts
0ml/2 tbsp lemon juice
lt

1 Top and tail the green beans and
cut into small pieces. Cook the
eans in the salted, boiling water for
–4 minutes. Drain the beans and
eserve the cooking water.

2 Spoon off 45–60ml/3–4 tbsp of
the cream from the top of the
oconut milk and reserve it.

3 Grind the garlic, nuts, *terasi*, and
ground coriander together to a
paste in a food processor or with a
pestle and mortar.

4 Heat the oil in a wok or saucepan,
and fry the onion until transparent.
Remove and reserve. Fry the paste for
2 minutes without browning. Pour in
the reserved vegetable water and
coconut milk. Bring to the boil and
add the *duan salam* or bay leaves. Cook,
uncovered, for 15–20 minutes.

5 Just before serving, add the beans,
fried onion, beansprouts, reserved
coconut cream and lemon juice. Taste
for seasoning and adjust it, if necessary.
Serve at once.

--- COOK'S TIP ---

Even in the East, cooks use canned
coconut milk. Any leftovers can be chilled
for 3–4 days or frozen immediately, then
thawed before use.

FISH
AND
SHELLFISH

There is a seemingly endless variety of fish available in Indonesian markets. I went to Jakarta's answer to Billingsgate, where oil-skinned and wellington-clad young men carried enormous baskets of fish on bamboo poles to the auction area. Mackerel, tuna, mullet, ikan merah (snapper) and cumi (squid) all feature, as well as superb shellfish, crabs and huge prawns. These recipes illustrate the delicious variety of Indonesian fish cuisine. Serving quantities assume you will be eating them as main courses, perhaps with rice and a salad or vegetable accompaniment. They will serve more people as part of a buffet.

Spicy Fish

If you make *Ikan Kecap* a day ahead, put it straight on to a serving dish after cooking and then pour over the sauce, cover and chill until required.

INGREDIENTS

Serves 3–4

450g/1lb fish fillets, such as mackerel,
   cod or haddock
30ml/2 tbsp plain flour
groundnut oil for frying
1 onion, roughly chopped
1 small garlic clove, crushed
4cm/1½in fresh root ginger, peeled
   and grated
1–2 fresh red chillies, seeded and sliced
1cm/½in cube *terasi*, prepared
60ml/4 tbsp water
juice of ½ lemon
15ml/1 tbsp brown sugar
30ml/2 tbsp dark soy sauce
salt
roughly torn lettuce leaves, to serve

1 Rinse the fish fillets under cold water and dry well on absorbent kitchen paper. Cut into serving portions and remove any bones.

2 Season the flour with salt and use it to dust the fish. Heat the oil in a frying pan and fry the fish on both sides for 3–4 minutes, or until cooked. Lift on to a plate and set aside.

3 Rinse out and dry the pan. Heat a little more oil and fry the onion, garlic, ginger and chillies just to bring out the flavour. Do not brown.

4 Blend the *terasi* with a little water, to make a paste. Add it to the onion mixture, with a little extra water if necessary. Cook for 2 minutes and then stir in the lemon juice, brown sugar and soy sauce.

5 Pour over the fish and serve, hot or cold, with roughly torn lettuce.

--- COOK'S TIP ---

For a buffet dish cut the fish into bite-size pieces or serving portions.

Squid from Madura

This squid dish, *Cumi Cumi Madura*, is popular in Indonesia. It is quite usual to be invited into the restaurant kitchen and given a warm welcome.

INGREDIENTS

Serves 2–3

450g/1lb cleaned and drained squid,
   body cut in strips, tentacles left whole
3 garlic cloves
1.5ml/¼ tsp ground nutmeg
1 bunch of spring onions
60ml/4 tbsp sunflower oil
250ml/8fl oz/1 cup water
15ml/1 tbsp dark soy sauce
salt and freshly ground black pepper
1 lime, cut in wedges (optional)
boiled rice, to serve

1 Squeeze out the little central "bone" from each tentacle. Heat a wok, toss in all the squid and stir-fry for 1 minute. Remove the squid.

2 Crush the garlic with the nutmeg and some salt and pepper. Trim the roots from the spring onions, cut the white part into small pieces, slice the green part and then set aside.

3 Heat the wok, add the oil and fry the white part of the spring onions. Stir in the garlic paste and the squid.

4 Rinse out the garlic paste container with the water and soy sauce and add to the pan. Half-cover and simmer for 4–5 minutes. Add the spring onion tops, toss lightly and serve at once, with lime, if using, and rice.

Whole Fish with Sweet and Sour Sauce

INGREDIENTS

Serves 4

1 whole fish, such as red snapper or
    carp, about 1kg/2¼lb
30–45ml/2–3 tbsp cornflour
oil for frying
salt and freshly ground black pepper
boiled rice, to serve

For the spice paste

2 garlic cloves
2 lemon grass stems
2.5cm/1in fresh *lengkuas*
2.5cm/1in fresh root ginger
2cm/¾in fresh turmeric or 2.5ml/
    ½ tsp ground turmeric
5 macadamia nuts or 10 almonds

For the sauce

15ml/1 tbsp brown sugar
45ml/3 tbsp cider vinegar
about 350ml/12fl oz/1½ cups water
2 lime leaves, torn
4 shallots, quartered
3 tomatoes, skinned and cut in wedges
3 spring onions, finely shredded
1 fresh red chilli, seeded and shredded

1 Ask the fishmonger to gut and
scale the fish, leaving on the head
and tail, or you may do this yourself.
Wash and dry the fish thoroughly and
then sprinkle it inside and out with salt.
Set aside for 15 minutes, while
preparing the other ingredients.

2 Peel and crush the garlic cloves.
Use only the lower white part of
the lemon grass stems and slice thinly.
Peel and slice the fresh *lengkuas*, the
fresh root ginger and fresh turmeric, if
using. Grind the nuts, garlic, lemon
grass, *lengkuas*, ginger and turmeric to a
fine paste in a food processor or with a
pestle and mortar.

3 Scrape the paste into a bowl. Stir
in the brown sugar, cider vinegar,
seasoning to taste and the water. Add
the lime leaves.

4 Dust the fish with the cornflour
and fry on both sides in hot oil for
about 8–9 minutes or until almost
cooked through. Drain the fish on
kitchen paper and transfer to a serving
dish. Keep warm.

5 Pour off most of the oil and then
pour in the spicy liquid and allow
to come to the boil. Reduce the heat
and cook for 3–4 minutes. Add the
shallots and tomatoes, followed a
minute later by the spring onions and
chilli. Taste and adjust the seasoning.

6 Pour the sauce over the fish. Serv
at once, with plenty of rice.

Spicy Squid

This aromatically spiced squid dish, *Cumi Cumi Smoor*, is a favourite in Madura, and is simple yet delicious. Gone are the days when cleaning squid was such a chore: now they can be bought ready-cleaned and are available from fish shops, market stalls or from the freezer or fish counters of large supermarkets.

INGREDIENTS

Serves 3–4

675g/1½lb squid, rinsed and drained
45ml/3 tbsp groundnut oil
1 onion, finely chopped
2 garlic cloves, crushed
1 beef tomato, skinned and chopped
15ml/1 tbsp dark soy sauce
2.5ml/½ tsp ground nutmeg
6 whole cloves
150ml/¼ pint/⅔ cup water
juice of ½ lemon or lime
salt and freshly ground black pepper
boiled rice, to serve

1 Cut squid into ribbons and remove the "bone" from each tentacle.

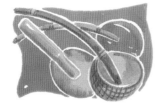

2 Heat a wok, toss in the squid and stir constantly for 2–3 minutes, when the squid will have curled into attractive shapes or into firm rings. Lift out and set aside in a warm place.

3 Heat the oil in a clean pan and fry the onion and garlic, until soft and beginning to brown. Add the tomato, soy sauce, nutmeg, cloves, water and lemon or lime juice. Bring to the boil and then reduce the heat and add the squid with seasoning to taste.

4 Cook gently for a further 3–5 minutes, uncovered, stirring from time to time. Take care not to overcook the squid. Serve hot or warm, with boiled rice, or as part of a buffet spread.

VARIATION

Instead of squid try using 450g/1lb cooked and peeled tiger prawns in this recipe. Add them for the final 1–2 minutes.

Prawns with Chayote in Turmeric Sauce

This delicious, attractively coloured dish is called *Gule Udang Dengan Labu Kuning*.

Ingredients

Serves 4
1–2 chayotes or 2–3 courgettes
2 fresh red chillies, seeded
1 onion, quartered
5mm/¼in fresh *lengkuas*, peeled
1 lemon grass stem, lower 5cm/2in
 sliced, top bruised
2.5cm/1in fresh turmeric, peeled
200ml/7fl oz/scant 1 cup water
lemon juice
400ml/14fl oz can coconut milk
450g/1lb cooked, peeled prawns
salt
red chilli shreds, to garnish (optional)
boiled rice, to serve

1 Peel the chayotes, remove the seeds and cut into strips. If using courgettes, cut into 5cm/2in strips.

2 Grind the fresh red chillies, onion, sliced *lengkuas*, sliced lemon grass and the fresh turmeric to a paste in a food processor or with a pestle and mortar. Add the water to the paste mixture, with a squeeze of lemon juice and salt to taste.

3 Pour into a pan. Add the top of the lemon grass stem. Bring to the boil and cook for 1–2 minutes. Add the chayote or courgette pieces and cook for 2 minutes. Stir in the coconut milk. Taste and adjust the seasoning.

4 Stir in the prawns and cook gently for 2–3 minutes. Remove the lemon grass stem. Garnish with shreds of chilli, if using, and serve with rice.

Doedoeh of Fish

Haddock or cod fillet may be substituted in this recipe.

Ingredients

Serves 6–8
1kg/2¼lb fresh mackerel
 fillets, skinned
30ml/2 tbsp tamarind pulp, soaked in
 200ml/7fl oz/scant 1 cup water
1 onion
1cm/½in fresh *lengkuas*
2 garlic cloves
1–2 fresh red chillies, seeded, or 5ml/
 1 tsp chilli powder
5ml/1 tsp ground coriander
5ml/1 tsp ground turmeric
2.5ml/½ tsp ground fennel seeds
15ml/1 tbsp dark brown sugar
90–105ml/6–7 tbsp oil
200ml/7fl oz/scant 1 cup
 coconut cream
salt and freshly ground black pepper
fresh chilli shreds, to garnish

1 Rinse the fish fillets in cold water and dry them well on kitchen paper. Put into a shallow dish and sprinkle with a little salt. Strain the tamarind and pour the juice over the fish fillets. Leave for 30 minutes.

2 Quarter the onion, peel and slice the *lengkuas* and peel the garlic. Grind the onion, *lengkuas*, garlic and chillies or chilli powder to a paste in a food processor or with a pestle and mortar. Add the ground coriander, turmeric, fennel seeds and sugar.

3 Heat half of the oil in a frying pan. Drain the fish fillets and fry for 5 minutes, or until cooked. Set aside.

4 Wipe out the pan and heat the remaining oil. Fry the spice paste, stirring all the time, until it gives off a spicy aroma. Do not let it brown. Add the coconut cream and simmer gently for a few minutes. Add the fish fillets and gently heat through.

5 Taste for seasoning and serve sprinkled with shredded chilli.

Chilli Crabs

It is possible to find variations on *Kepitang Pedas* all over Asia. It will be memorable whether you eat in simple surroundings or in a sophisticated restaurant.

INGREDIENTS

Serves 4

2 cooked crabs, about 675g/1½lb
1cm/½in cube *terasi*
2 garlic cloves
2 fresh red chillies, seeded, or 5ml/
   1 tsp chopped chilli from a jar
1cm/½in fresh root ginger, peeled
   and sliced
60ml/4 tbsp sunflower oil
300ml/½ pint/1¼ cups tomato ketchup
15ml/1 tbsp dark brown sugar
150ml/¼ pint/⅔ cup warm water
4 spring onions, chopped, to garnish
cucumber chunks and hot toast,
   to serve (optional)

1 Remove the large claws of one crab and turn on to its back, with the head facing away from you. Use your thumbs to push the body up from the main shell. Discard the stomach sac and "dead men's fingers", i.e. lungs and any green matter. Leave the creamy brown meat in the shell and cut the shell in half, with a cleaver or strong knife. Cut the body section in half and crack the claws with a sharp blow from a hammer or cleaver. Avoid splintering the claws. Repeat with the other crab.

2 Grind the *terasi*, garlic, chillies and ginger to a paste in a food processor or with a pestle and mortar.

3 Heat a wok and add the oil. Fry the spice paste, stirring it all the time, without browning.

4 Stir in the tomato ketchup, sugar and water and mix the sauce well. When just boiling, add all the crab pieces and toss in the sauce until well-coated and hot. Serve in a large bowl, sprinkled with the spring onions. Place in the centre of the table for everyone to help themselves. Accompany this finger-licking dish with cool cucumber chunks and hot toast for mopping up the sauce, if you like.

Boemboe Bali of Fish

The island of Bali has wonderful fish, surrounded as it is by sparkling blue sea. This simple fish "curry" is packed with many of the characteristic flavours associated with Indonesia.

INGREDIENTS

Serves 4–6

675g/1½lb cod or haddock fillet
1cm/½in cube *terasi*
2 red or white onions
2.5cm/1in fresh root ginger, peeled and sliced
1cm/½in fresh *lengkuas*, peeled and sliced, or 5ml/1 tsp *lengkuas* powder
2 garlic cloves
1–2 fresh red chillies, seeded, or 10ml/2 tsp Chilli Sambal, or 5–10ml/1–2 tsp chilli powder
90ml/6 tbsp sunflower oil
15ml/1 tbsp dark soy sauce
5ml/1 tsp tamarind pulp, soaked in 30ml/2 tbsp warm water
250ml/8fl oz/1 cup water
celery leaves or chopped fresh chilli, to garnish
boiled rice, to serve

1 Skin the fish, remove any bones and then cut the flesh into bite-size pieces. Pat dry with kitchen paper and set aside.

2 Grind the *terasi*, onions, ginger, *lengkuas*, garlic and fresh chillies, if using, to a paste in a food processor or with a pestle and mortar. Stir in the Chilli Sambal or chilli powder and *lengkuas* powder, if using.

3 Heat 30ml/2 tbsp of the oil and fry the spice mixture, stirring, until it gives off a rich aroma. Add the soy sauce. Strain the tamarind and add the juice and water. Cook for 2–3 minutes.

--- VARIATION ---

Substitute 450g/1lb cooked tiger prawns. Add them 3 minutes before the end.

4 In a separate pan, fry the fish in the remaining oil for 2–3 minutes. Turn once only so that the pieces stay whole. Lift out with a draining spoon and put into the sauce.

5 Cook the fish in the sauce for a further 3 minutes and serve with boiled rice. Garnish with feathery celery leaves or a little chopped fresh chilli, if you like.

Baked or Grilled Spiced Whole Fish

INGREDIENTS

Serves 6

1kg/2¼lb bream, carp or pomfret, cleaned and scaled if necessary
1 fresh red chilli, seeded and ground, or 5ml/1 tsp chopped chilli from a jar
4 garlic cloves, crushed
2.5cm/1in fresh root ginger, peeled and sliced
4 spring onions, chopped
juice of ½ lemon
30ml/2 tbsp sunflower oil
salt
boiled rice, to serve

1 Rinse the fish and dry it well inside and out with absorbent kitchen paper. Slash two or three times through the fleshy part on each side of the fish.

2 Place the chilli, garlic, ginger and spring onions in a food processor and blend to a paste, or grind the mixture together with a pestle and mortar. Add the lemon juice and salt, then stir in the oil.

3 Spoon a little of the mixture inside the fish and pour the rest over the top. Turn the fish to coat it completely in the spice mixture and leave to marinate for at least an hour.

4 Preheat the grill. Place a long strip of double foil under the fish to support it and to make turning it over easier. Put on a rack in a grill pan and cook under the hot grill for 5 minutes on one side and 8 minutes on the second side, basting with the marinade during cooking. Serve with boiled rice.

Vinegar Fish

INGREDIENTS

Serves 2–3

2–3 mackerel, filleted
2–3 fresh red chillies, seeded
4 macadamia nuts or 8 almonds
1 red onion, quartered
2 garlic cloves, crushed
1cm/½in fresh root ginger, peeled and sliced
5ml/1 tsp ground turmeric
45ml/3 tbsp coconut or vegetable oil
45ml/3 tbsp wine vinegar
150ml/¼ pint/⅔ cup water
salt
Deep-fried Onions, to garnish
finely chopped fresh chilli, to garnish

1 Rinse the fish fillets in cold water and then dry them well on kitchen paper. Set aside.

2 Grind the chillies, nuts, onion, garlic, ginger, turmeric and 15ml/1 tbsp of the oil to a paste in a food processor or with a pestle and mortar. Heat the remaining oil in a frying pan and cook the paste for 1–2 minutes, without browning. Stir in the vinegar and water. Add salt to taste. Bring to the boil, then reduce to a simmer.

3 Place the fish fillets in the sauce. Cover and cook for 6–8 minutes, or until the fish is tender.

4 Lift the fish on to a plate and keep warm. Reduce the sauce by boiling rapidly for 1 minute. Pour over the fish and serve. Garnish with Deep-fried Onions and chopped chilli.

MEAT
AND
POULTRY

*Meat is expensive in Indonesia, so with more than a
touch of skill and ingenuity a little is made to go a
long way, by adding vegetables, rice and so on.
Chicken is very popular. In many recipes chicken is
marinated or cooked in a variety of "wet" spices,
lengkuas, lemon grass, turmeric and frequently
coconut milk, which transform the humble bird
into something special. Ducks are also commonly used
and Balinese Spiced Duck is especially characteristic.
The substantial Chinese population has contributed
some delicious duck recipes and it is also responsible for
the few dishes that use pork, which is not widely eaten
in this primarily Islamic country. Rendang is one of the
most popular and well-known Indonesian dishes.*

Rendang

INGREDIENTS

Serves 6–8

1kg/2¼ lb prime beef in one piece
2 onions or 5–6 shallots, sliced
4 garlic cloves, crushed
2.5cm/1in fresh *lengkuas*, peeled and
  sliced, or 5ml/1 tsp *lengkuas* powder
2.5cm/1in fresh root ginger, peeled
  and sliced
4–6 fresh red chillies, seeded and sliced
1 lemon grass stem, lower part, sliced
2.5cm/1in fresh turmeric, peeled and
  sliced, or 5ml/1 tsp ground turmeric
5ml/1 tsp coriander seeds, dry-fried
  and ground
5ml/1 tsp cumin seeds, dry-fried
  and ground
2 lime leaves
5ml/1 tsp tamarind pulp, soaked in
  60ml/4 tbsp warm water
2 x 400ml/14fl oz cans coconut milk
300ml/½ pint/1¼ cups water
30ml/2 tbsp dark soy sauce
8 small new potatoes, scrubbed
salt
Deep-fried Onions, to garnish

1 Cut the meat in long strips and then into pieces of even size and place in a bowl.

2 Grind the onions or shallots, garlic, *lengkuas* or *lengkuas* powder, ginger, chillies, sliced lemon grass and turmeric to a fine paste in a food processor or with a pestle and mortar.

3 Add the paste to the meat with the coriander and cumin and mix well. Tear the lime leaves and add them to the mixture. Cover and leave in a cool place to marinate while you prepare the other ingredients.

4 Strain the tamarind and reserve the juice. Pour the coconut milk, water and the tamarind juice into a wok or flameproof casserole and stir in the spiced meat and soy sauce. Add seasoning as desired.

5 Stir until the liquid comes to the boil and then reduce the heat and simmer gently, half-covered, for about 1½–2 hours or until the meat is tender and the liquid reduced.

6 Add the potatoes 20–25 minutes before the end of the cooking time. They will absorb some of the sauce, so add a little more water to compensate for this, if you prefer the Rendang to be rather moister than it would be in Indonesia.

7 Adjust the seasoning and transfer to a serving bowl. Serve garnished with the crisp Deep-fried Onions.

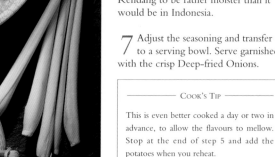

COOK'S TIP

This is even better cooked a day or two in advance, to allow the flavours to mellow. Stop at the end of step 5 and add the potatoes when you reheat.

Grilled Chicken

he flavour of this dish, known
 Indonesia as *Ayam Bakur*, will
 more intense if the chicken is
arinated overnight. It is an
eal recipe for a party, because
e final grilling, barbecuing or
king can be done at the last
inute. Poussin portions will
ok even more attractive, but
member that they will need less
ooking time than chicken
iarters, for instance. Sweet and
ur Fruit and Vegetable Salad
akes a perfect accompaniment
r this grilled chicken dish.

GREDIENTS

rves 4

5kg/3–3½lb chicken or
2 poussins
garlic cloves, crushed
emon grass stems, lower 5cm/
2in sliced
m/½ in fresh *lengkuas*, peeled
and sliced
nl/1 tsp ground turmeric
'5ml/16fl oz/2 cups water
-4 bay leaves
ml/3 tbsp each dark and light
soy sauce
g/2oz butter or margarine
t
iled rice, to serve

1 Cut the chicken into four or eight
 portions. Halve the poussins or quarter
em, if you are serving this as part of a
iffet. Slash the fleshy part of each
rtion twice and set aside.

2 Grind the garlic, sliced lemon
 grass, *lengkuas*, turmeric and
salt together into a paste in a food
processor or with a pestle and mortar.
Rub the paste into the chicken pieces
and leave for at least 30 minutes. Wear
rubber gloves for this, as the turmeric
will stain heavily; or wash your hands
immediately after mixing, if you prefer.

3 Transfer the chicken or poussin
 pieces to a wok and pour in the
water. Add the bay leaves and bring to
the boil. Cover and cook gently for 30
minutes, adding a little more water if
necessary. Stir from time to time.

4 Just before serving, add the two
 soy sauces to the pan together with
the butter or margarine.

5 Cook until the chicken or poussin
 is well-coated and the sauce
has almost been absorbed. Transfer
the chicken or poussin pieces to a
preheated grill or barbecue, or an oven
preheated to 200°C/400°F/ Gas 6,
to finish cooking. Cook for a further
10–15 minutes, turning the pieces
often so they become golden brown all
over. Take care not to let them burn.
Baste with the remaining sauce during
cooking. Serve with boiled rice.

Chicken with Turmeric

INGREDIENTS

Serves 4

1.5kg/3–3½lb chicken, cut in 8 pieces,
  or 4 chicken quarters, each halved
15ml/1 tbsp sugar
3 macadamia nuts or 6 almonds
2 garlic cloves, crushed
1 large onion, quartered
2.5cm/1in fresh *lengkuas*, peeled and
  sliced, or 5ml/1 tsp *lengkuas* powder
1–2 lemon grass stems, lower 5cm/2in
  sliced, top bruised
1cm/½in cube *terasi*
4cm/1½in fresh turmeric, peeled and
  sliced, or 15ml/1 tbsp
  ground turmeric
15ml/1 tbsp tamarind pulp, soaked in
  150ml/¼ pint/⅔ cup warm water
60–90ml/4–6 tbsp oil
400ml/14fl oz/1⅔ cups coconut milk
salt and freshly ground black pepper
Deep-fried Onions, to garnish

1 Rub the chicken joints with a little sugar and set them aside.

2 Grind the nuts and garlic in a food processor with the onion, *lengkuas*, sliced lemon grass, *terasi*, and turmeric. Alternatively, pound the ingredients to a paste with a pestle and mortar. Strain the tamarind pulp and reserve the juice.

3 Heat the oil in a wok and cook th paste, without browning, until it gives off a spicy aroma. Add the piece of chicken and toss well in the spices. Add the strained tamarind juice. Spoo the coconut cream off the top of the milk and set it to one side.

4 Add the coconut milk to the pan. Cover and cook for 45 minutes, c until the chicken is tender.

5 Just before serving, stir in the coconut cream while coming to the boil. Season and serve at once, garnished with Deep-fried Onions.

Chicken Cooked in Coconut Milk

raditionally, the chicken pieces vould be part-cooked by frying, ut I think that roasting in the ven is a better option. *Ayam Opor* is an unusual recipe in that he sauce is white as it does not ontain chillies or turmeric, nlike many other Indonesian ishes. The dish is served with risp Deep-fried Onions.

NGREDIENTS

erves 4

.5kg/3–3½ lb chicken or
  4 chicken quarters
- garlic cloves
 onion, sliced
- macadamia nuts or 8 almonds
5ml/1 tbsp coriander seeds, dry-fried,
  or 5ml/1 tsp ground coriander
5ml/3 tbsp oil
.5cm/1in fresh *lengkuas*, peeled
  and bruised
lemon grass stems, fleshy part bruised
lime leaves
bay leaves
ml/1 tsp sugar
00ml/1 pint/2½ cups coconut milk
alt
oiled rice and Deep-fried Onions,
  to serve

1 Preheat the oven to 190°C/375°F/ Gas 5. Cut the chicken into four r eight pieces. Season with salt. Put in n oiled roasting tin and cook in the ven for 25–30 minutes. Meanwhile repare the sauce.

2 Grind the garlic, onion, nuts and coriander to a fine paste in a food processor or with a pestle and mortar. Heat the oil and fry the paste to bring out the flavour. Do not allow it to brown.

3 Add the part-cooked chicken pieces to a wok together with the *lengkuas*, lemon grass, lime and bay leaves, sugar, coconut milk and salt to taste. Mix well to coat in the sauce.

4 Bring to the boil and then reduce the heat and simmer gently for 30–40 minutes, uncovered, until the chicken is tender and the coconut sauce is reduced and thickened. Stir the mixture occasionally during cooking.

5 Just before serving remove the bruised *lengkuas* and lemon grass. Serve with boiled rice sprinkled with crisp Deep-fried Onions.

Aromatic Chicken from Madura

Magadip is best cooked ahead so that the flavours permeate the chicken flesh making it even more delicious. A cool cucumber salad is a good accompaniment.

INGREDIENTS

Serves 4

1.5kg/3–3½lb chicken, cut in quarters, or 4 chicken quarters
5ml/1 tsp sugar
30ml/2 tbsp coriander seeds
10ml/2 tsp cumin seeds
6 whole cloves
2.5ml/½ tsp ground nutmeg
2.5ml/½ tsp ground turmeric
1 small onion
2.5cm/1in fresh root ginger, peeled and sliced
300ml/½ pint/1¼ cups chicken stock or water
salt and freshly ground black pepper
boiled rice and Deep-fried Onions, to serve

1 Cut each chicken quarter in half to obtain eight pieces. Place in a flameproof casserole, sprinkle with sugar and salt and toss together. This helps release the juices in the chicken. Use the backbone and any remaining carcass to make chicken stock for use later in the recipe, if you like.

——— COOK'S TIP ———

Add a large piece of bruised ginger and a small onion to the chicken stock to ensure a good flavour.

2 Dry-fry the coriander, cumin and whole cloves until the spices give off a good aroma. Add the nutmeg and turmeric and heat briefly. Grind in a food processor or a pestle and mortar.

3 If using a processor, process the onion and ginger until finely chopped. Otherwise, finely chop the onion and ginger and pound to a paste with a pestle and mortar. Add the spices and stock or water and mix well.

4 Pour over the chicken in the flameproof casserole. Cover with a lid and cook over a gentle heat until the chicken pieces are really tender, about 45–50 minutes.

5 Serve portions of the chicken, with the sauce, on boiled rice, scattered with crisp Deep-fried Onions.

Chicken with Spices and Soy Sauce

A very simple recipe, called *Ayam Kecap,* which will often appear as one of the dishes on a Padang restaurant menu. Any leftovers taste equally good when reheated the following day.

INGREDIENTS

Serves 4

1.5kg/3–3½lb chicken, jointed and cut in 16 pieces
3 onions, sliced
about 1 litre/1¾ pints/4 cups water
4 garlic cloves, crushed
3–4 fresh red chillies, seeded and sliced, or 15ml/1 tbsp chilli powder
45–60ml/3–4 tbsp oil
2.5ml/½ tsp ground nutmeg
6 whole cloves
5ml/1 tsp tamarind pulp, soaked in 45ml/3 tbsp warm water
30–45ml/2–3 tbsp dark or light soy sauce
salt
fresh red chilli shreds, to garnish
boiled rice, to serve

1 Prepare the chicken and place the pieces in a large pan with one of the onions. Pour over enough water to just cover. Bring to the boil and then reduce the heat and simmer gently for 20 minutes.

2 Grind the remaining onions, with the garlic and chillies, to a fine paste in a food processor or with a pestle and mortar. Heat a little of the oil in a wok or frying pan and cook the paste to bring out the flavour, but do not allow to brown.

3 When the chicken has cooked for 20 minutes, lift it out of the stock in the pan using a draining spoon and put it straight into the spicy mixture. Toss everything together over a fairly high heat so that the spices permeate the chicken pieces. Reserve 300ml/ ½ pint/1¼ cups of the chicken stock to add to the pan later.

4 Stir in the nutmeg and cloves. Strain the tamarind and add the tamarind juice and the soy sauce to the chicken. Cook for a further 2–3 minutes, then add the reserved stock.

5 Taste and adjust the seasoning and cook, uncovered, for a further 25–35 minutes, until the chicken pieces are tender.

6 Serve the chicken in a bowl, topped with shredded chilli, and eat with boiled rice.

COOK'S TIP

Dark soy sauce is thicker and more salty than light. Adding the dark variety will give a deeper colour to the chicken.

Spicy Meat Fritters

INGREDIENTS

Makes 30

450g/1lb potatoes, boiled and drained
450g/1lb lean minced beef
1 onion, quartered
1 bunch spring onions, chopped
3 garlic cloves, crushed
5ml/1 tsp ground nutmeg
15ml/1 tbsp coriander seeds, dry-fried
  and ground
10ml/2 tsp cumin seeds, dry-fried
  and ground
4 eggs, beaten
oil for shallow-frying
salt and freshly ground black pepper

1 While the potatoes are still warm, mash them in the pan until they are well broken up. Add to the minced beef and mix well together.

2 Finely chop the onion, spring onions and garlic. Add to the meat with the ground nutmeg, coriander and cumin. Stir in enough beaten egg to give a soft consistency which can be formed into fritters. Season to taste.

3 Heat the oil in a large frying pan. Using a dessertspoon, scoop out 6–8 oval-shaped fritters and drop them into the hot oil. Allow to set, so that they keep their shape (this will take about 3 minutes) and then turn over and cook for a further minute.

4 Drain well on kitchen paper and keep warm while cooking the remaining fritters.

Barbecued Pork Spareribs

INGREDIENTS

Serves 4

1kg/2¼ lb pork spareribs
1 onion
2 garlic cloves
2.5cm/1in fresh root ginger
75ml/3fl oz/⅓ cup dark soy sauce
1–2 fresh red chillies, seeded
  and chopped
5ml/1 tsp tamarind pulp, soaked in
  75ml/3fl oz/⅓ cup water
15–30ml/1–2 tbsp dark brown sugar
30ml/2 tbsp groundnut oil
salt and freshly ground black pepper

1 Wipe the pork ribs and place them in a wok, wide frying pan or large flameproof casserole.

2 Finely chop the onion, crush the garlic and peel and slice the ginger. Blend the soy sauce, onion, garlic, ginger and chopped chillies together to a paste in a food processor or with a pestle and mortar. Strain the tamarind and reserve the juice. Add the tamarind juice, brown sugar, oil and seasoning to taste to the onion mixture and mix well together.

3 Pour the sauce over the ribs and toss well to coat. Bring to the boil and then simmer, uncovered and stirring frequently, for 30 minutes. Add extra water if necessary.

4 Put the ribs on a rack in a roasting tin, place under a preheated grill, on a barbecue or in the oven at 200°C/400°F/Gas 6 and continue cooking until the ribs are tender, about 20 minutes, depending on the thickness of the ribs. Baste the ribs with the sauce and turn them over from time to time.

Balinese Spiced Duck

There is a delightful hotel on the beach at Sanur which cooks this delicious duck dish perfectly.

INGREDIENTS

Serves 4

8 duck portions, fat trimmed
　and reserved
50g/2oz desiccated coconut
175ml/6fl oz/³/₄ cup coconut milk
salt and freshly ground black pepper
Deep-fried Onions and salad leaves or
　fresh herb sprigs, to garnish

For the spice paste

1 small onion or 4–6 shallots, sliced
2 garlic cloves, sliced
2.5cm/¹/₂in fresh root ginger, peeled
　and sliced
1cm/¹/₂in fresh *lengkuas*, peeled
　and sliced
2.5cm/1in fresh turmeric or 2.5ml/
　¹/₂ tsp ground turmeric
1–2 red chillies, seeded and sliced
4 macadamia nuts or 8 almonds
5ml/1 tsp coriander seeds, dry-fried

1 Place the duck fat trimmings in a heated frying pan, without oil, and allow the fat to render. Reserve the fat.

2 Dry-fry the desiccated coconut in a preheated pan until crisp and brown in colour.

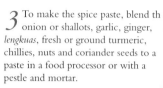

3 To make the spice paste, blend the onion or shallots, garlic, ginger, *lengkuas*, fresh or ground turmeric, chillies, nuts and coriander seeds to a paste in a food processor or with a pestle and mortar.

4 Spread the spice paste over the duck portions and leave to marinate in a cool place for 3–4 hours. Preheat the oven to 160°C/325°F/ Gas 3. Shake off the spice paste and transfer the duck breasts to an oiled roasting tin. Cover with a double layer of foil and cook the duck in the oven for 2 hours.

5 Turn the oven temperature up to 190°C/375°F/Gas 5. Heat the reserved duck fat in a pan, add the spice paste and fry for 1–2 minutes. Stir in the coconut milk and simmer for 2 minutes. Discard the duck juices then cover the duck with the spice mixture and sprinkle with the toasted coconut. Cook in the oven for 20–30 minutes.

6 Arrange the duck on a warm serving platter and sprinkle with the Deep-fried Onions. Season to taste and serve with the salad leaves or fresh herb sprigs of your choice.

Duck with Chinese Mushrooms and Ginger

Ducks are often seen, comically herded in single file, along the water channels between the rice paddies throughout the country. The substantial Chinese population in Indonesia is particularly fond of duck and the delicious ingredients in this recipe give it an oriental flavour.

INGREDIENTS

Serves 4

2.5kg/5½lb duck
5ml/1 tsp sugar
60ml/2fl oz/¼ cup light soy sauce
2 garlic cloves, crushed
6 dried Chinese mushrooms, soaked in 350ml/12fl oz/1½ cups warm water for 15 minutes
1 onion, sliced
5cm/2in fresh root ginger, sliced and cut in matchsticks
200g/7oz baby sweetcorn
½ bunch spring onions, white bulbs left whole, green tops sliced
15–30ml/1–2 tbsp cornflour, mixed to a paste with 60ml/4 tbsp water
salt and freshly ground black pepper
boiled rice, to serve

1 Cut the duck along the breast, open it up and cut along each side of the backbone. Use the backbone, wings and giblets to make a stock, to use later in the recipe. Any trimmings of fat can be rendered in a frying pan, to use later in the recipe. Cut each leg and each breast in half. Place in a bowl, rub with the sugar and then pour over the soy sauce and garlic.

2 Drain the mushrooms, reserving the soaking liquid. Trim and discard the stalks.

3 Fry the onion and ginger in the duck fat, in a frying pan, until they give off a good aroma. Push to one side. Lift the duck pieces out of the soy sauce and fry them until browned. Add the mushrooms and reserved liquid.

4 Add 600ml/1 pint/2½ cups of the duck stock or water to the browned duck pieces. Season, cover and cook over a gentle heat for about 1 hour, until the duck is tender.

5 Add the sweetcorn and the white part of the spring onions and cook for a further 10 minutes. Remove from the heat and add the cornflour paste. Return to the heat and bring to the boil, stirring. Cook for 1 minute until glossy. Serve, scattered with the spring onion tops, with boiled rice.

VARIATION

Replace the corn with chopped celery and slices of drained, canned water chestnuts.

Spiced Chicken Sauté

INGREDIENTS

Serves 4

1.5kg/3–3½lb chicken, cut in 8 pieces
5ml/1 tsp each salt and freshly ground
  black pepper
2 garlic cloves, crushed
150ml/¼ pint/⅔ cup sunflower oil

For the sauce

25g/1oz butter
30ml/2 tbsp sunflower oil
1 onion, sliced
4 garlic cloves, crushed
2 large, ripe beefsteak tomatoes, sliced
  and chopped, or 400g/14oz can
  chopped tomatoes with
  chilli, drained
600ml/1 pint/2½ cups water
50ml/2fl oz/¼ cup dark soy sauce
salt and freshly ground black pepper
sliced fresh red chilli, to garnish
Deep-fried Onions, to
  garnish (optional)
boiled rice, to serve

1 Preheat the oven to 190°C/375°F/
Gas 5. Make two slashes in the
fleshy part of each chicken piece. Rub
well with the salt, pepper and garlic.
Drizzle with a little of the oil and bake
for 30 minutes, or shallow-fry, in hot
oil for 12–15 minutes, until brown.

2 To make the sauce, heat the butter
and oil in a wok and fry the onion
and garlic until soft. Add the tomatoes,
water, soy sauce and seasoning. Boil
briskly for 5 minutes, to reduce the
sauce and concentrate the flavour.

3 Add the chicken to the sauce in
the wok. Turn the chicken pieces
over in the sauce to coat them well.
Continue cooking slowly for about
20 minutes until the chicken pieces are
tender. Stir the mixture occasionally.

4 Arrange the chicken on a warm
serving platter and garnish with the
sliced chilli and Deep-fried Onions, if
using. Serve with boiled rice.

Stir-fried Chicken with Pineapple

INGREDIENTS

Serves 4–6

500g/1¼ lb boneless, skinless chicken
  breasts, thinly sliced at an angle
30ml/2 tbsp cornflour
60ml/4 tbsp sunflower oil
1 garlic clove, crushed
5cm/2in fresh root ginger, peeled and
  cut in matchsticks
1 small onion, thinly sliced
1 fresh pineapple, peeled, cored and
  cubed, or 425g/15oz can pineapple
  chunks in natural juice
30ml/2 tbsp dark soy sauce or
  15ml/1 tbsp *kecap manis*
1 bunch spring onions, white bulbs left
  whole, green tops sliced
salt and freshly ground black pepper

1 Toss the strips of chicken in the
cornflour with a little seasoning.
Fry in hot oil until tender.

2 Lift out of the wok or frying pan
and keep warm. Reheat the oil and
fry the garlic, ginger and onion until
soft, but not browned. Add the fresh
pineapple and 120ml/4fl oz/½ cup
water, or the canned pineapple pieces
together with their juice.

3 Stir in the soy sauce or *kecap manis*
and return the chicken to the pan
to heat through.

4 Taste and adjust the seasoning. Stir
in the whole spring onion bulbs
and half of the sliced green tops. Toss
well together and then turn the
chicken stir-fry on to a serving platter.
Serve garnished with the remaining
sliced green spring onions.

Spicy Meatballs

Serve *Pergedel Djawa* with either
a *sambal* or spicy sauce.

INGREDIENTS

Makes 24
1 large onion, roughly chopped
1–2 fresh red chillies, seeded
  and chopped
2 garlic cloves, crushed
1cm/½in cube *terasi*, prepared
15ml/1 tbsp coriander seeds
5ml/1 tsp cumin seeds
450g/1lb lean minced beef
10ml/2 tsp dark soy sauce
5ml/1 tsp dark brown sugar
juice of ½ lemon
a little beaten egg
oil for shallow-frying
salt and freshly ground black pepper
fresh coriander sprigs, to garnish

1 Put the onion, chillies, garlic and *terasi* in a food processor. Process but do not over-chop or the onion will become too wet and spoil the consistency of the meatballs. Dry-fry the coriander and cumin seeds in a preheated pan for about 1 minute, to release the aroma. Do not brown. Grind with a pestle and mortar.

2 Put the meat in a large bowl. Stir in the onion mixture. Add the ground coriander and cumin, soy sauce, seasoning, sugar and lemon juice. Bind with a little beaten egg and shape into small, even-size balls.

3 Chill the meatballs briefly to firm up, if necessary. Fry in shallow oil, turning often, until cooked through and browned. This will take 4–5 minutes, depending on their size.

4 Remove from the pan, drain well on kitchen paper and serve, garnished with coriander sprigs.

Beef and Aubergine Curry

INGREDIENTS

Serves 6

120ml/4fl oz/½ cup sunflower oil
3 onions, thinly sliced
2.5cm/1in fresh root ginger, sliced and
    cut in matchsticks
1 garlic clove, crushed
2 fresh red chillies, seeded and very
    finely sliced
2.5cm/1in fresh turmeric, peeled and
    crushed, or 5ml/1 tsp
    ground turmeric
1 lemon grass stem, lower part sliced
    finely, top bruised
675g/1½ lb braising steak, cut in even-
    size strips
400ml/14fl oz can coconut milk
300ml/½ pint/1¼ cups water
1 aubergine, sliced and patted dry
5ml/1 tsp tamarind pulp, soaked in
    60ml/4 tbsp warm water
salt and freshly ground black pepper
finely sliced chilli, (optional) and Deep-
    fried Onions, to garnish
boiled rice, to serve

1 Heat half the oil and fry the
onions, ginger and garlic until they
give off a rich aroma. Add the chillies,
turmeric and the lower part of the
lemon grass. Push to one side and then
turn up the heat and add the steak,
stirring until the meat changes colour.

COOK'S TIP

If you want to make this curry, *Gulai
Terung Dengan Daging,* ahead, prepare to
the end of step 2 and finish later.

---

2 Add the coconut milk, water,
lemon grass top and seasoning to
taste. Cover and simmer gently for
1½ hours, or until the meat is tender.

3 Towards the end of the cooking
time heat the remaining oil in a
frying pan. Fry the aubergine slices
until brown on both sides.

4 Add the browned aubergine slices
to the beef curry and cook for a
further 15 minutes. Stir gently from
time to time. Strain the tamarind and
stir the juice into the curry. Taste and
adjust the seasoning. Put into a warm
serving dish. Garnish with the sliced
chilli, if using, and Deep-fried Onions,
and serve with boiled rice.

SAMBALS AND PICKLES

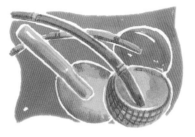

A sambal or sambalan is a sauce or dip that is placed on the table to give extra flavour to a saté. Sambal Kecap or Chilli Sambal can be used to pep up soups and is used in making spice pastes. Sambal Goreng is a chilli-spiced sauce to which coconut cream is added. A few minutes before serving, a variety of cooked ingredients, from prawns to chicken livers, hard-boiled eggs or vegetables, are added to the sauce. It is a really useful basic sauce, rather like our tomato or cheese sauces, which can be used to dress up different ingredients in a variety of ways. Acar or atjar is a side dish with either a sweet-sour or a turmeric-based dressing, not unlike a piccalilli.

Sambal Kecap

This can be served as a dip for *satés* instead of the usual peanut sauce and is particularly good with beef and chicken *satés* and deep-fried chicken.

INGREDIENTS

Makes about 150ml/¼ pint/⅔ cup
1 fresh red chilli, seeded and
   chopped finely
2 garlic cloves, crushed
60ml/4 tbsp dark soy sauce
20ml/4 tsp lemon juice, or
   15–25ml/1–1½ tbsp prepared
   tamarind juice
30ml/2 tbsp hot water
30ml/2 tbsp Deep-fried Onions
   (optional)

1 Mix the chilli, garlic, soy sauce, lemon or tamarind juice and hot water together in a bowl.

2 Stir in the Deep-fried Onions, if using, and leave to stand for 30 minutes before serving.

Deep-fried Onions

Known as *Bawang Goreng,* these are a traditional accompaniment and garnish to many Indonesian dishes. Oriental stores sell them ready-prepared, but it is simple to make them at home, using fresh onions, or for an even faster way, use a 75g/3oz packet of quick-dried onions, which you can fry in about 250ml/8fl oz/ 1 cup of sunflower oil. This gives you 115g/4oz of fried onion flakes. The small red onions that can be bought in Asian shops are excellent when deep-fried as they contain less water than most European varieties.

INGREDIENTS

Makes 450g/1lb
450g/1lb onions
oil for deep-frying

1 Peel and slice the onions as evenly and finely as possible.

2 Spread out thinly on kitchen paper, in an airy place, and leave to dry for 30 minutes–2 hours.

3 Heat the oil in deep-fryer or wok to 190°C/375°F. Fry the onions in batches, until crisp and golden, turning all the time. Drain well on kitchen paper and cool. Deep-fried Onions may be stored in an airtight container.

COOK'S TIP

Garlic can be prepared and cooked in the same way, or some can be fried with the last batch of onions. Deep-fried Garlic gives an added dimension in flavour as a garnish for many dishes.

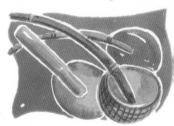

Sambal Goreng

Traditional flavourings for this dish are fine strips of calves' liver, chicken livers, green beans or hard-boiled eggs. A westernized version is shown here.

INGREDIENTS

Makes 900ml/1½ pints/3¾ cups

2.5cm/1in cube *terasi*
2 onions, quartered
2 garlic cloves, crushed
2.5cm/1in fresh *lengkuas*, peeled and sliced
10ml/2 tsp Chilli Sambal or 2 fresh red chillies, seeded and sliced
1.5ml/¼ tsp salt
30ml/2 tbsp oil
45ml/3 tbsp tomato purée
600ml/1 pint/2½ cups stock or water
60ml/4 tbsp tamarind juice
pinch sugar
45ml/3 tbsp coconut milk or cream

1 Grind the *terasi*, with the onions and garlic, to a paste in a food processor or with a pestle and mortar. Add the *lengkuas*, Chilli Sambal or sliced chillies and salt. Process or pound to a fine paste.

2 Fry the paste in hot oil for 1–2 minutes, without browning, until the mixture gives off a rich aroma.

3 Add the tomato purée and the stock or water and cook for about 10 minutes. Add 350g/12oz cooked chicken pieces and 50g/2oz cooked and sliced French beans, or one of the flavouring variations below, to half the quantity of the sauce. Cook in the sauce for 3–4 minutes, then stir in the tamarind juice, sugar and coconut milk or cream at the last minute, before tasting and serving.

VARIATIONS

Tomato *Sambal Goreng* – Add 450g/1lb of skinned, seeded and coarsely chopped tomatoes, before the stock.

Prawn *Sambal Goreng* – Add 350g/12oz cooked, peeled prawns and 1 green pepper, seeded and chopped.

Egg *Sambal Goreng* – Add 3 or 4 hard-boiled eggs, shelled and chopped, and 2 tomatoes, skinned, seeded and chopped.

Mixed Vegetable Pickle

If you can obtain fresh turmeric, it makes such a difference to the colour and appearance of *Acar Campur*. You can use almost any vegetable, bearing in mind that you need a balance of textures, flavours and colours.

INGREDIENTS

Makes 2–3 x 300g/11oz jars
1 fresh red chilli, seeded and sliced
1 onion, quartered
3 garlic cloves, crushed
1cm/½ in cube *terasi*
6 macadamia nuts or 8 almonds
2.5cm/1in fresh turmeric, peeled and sliced, or 5ml/1 tsp ground turmeric
60ml/2fl oz/¼ cup sunflower oil
475ml/16fl oz/2 cups white vinegar
250ml/8fl oz/1 cup water
25–50g/1–2oz granulated sugar
3 carrots
225g/8oz green beans
1 small cauliflower
1 cucumber
225g/8oz white cabbage
115g/4oz dry-roasted peanuts, roughly crushed
salt

1 Place the chilli, onion, garlic, *terasi*, nuts and turmeric in a food processor and blend to a paste, or pound in a mortar with a pestle.

2 Heat the oil and stir-fry the paste to release the aroma. Add the vinegar, water, sugar and salt. Bring to the boil. Simmer for 10 minutes.

3 Cut the carrots into flower shapes. Cut the green beans into short, neat lengths. Separate the cauliflower into neat, bite-size florets. Peel and seed the cucumber and cut the flesh in neat, bite-size pieces. Cut the cabbage in neat, bite-size pieces.

4 Blanch each vegetable separately, in a large pan of boiling water, for 1 minute. Transfer to a colander and rinse with cold water, to halt the cooking. Drain well.

— COOK'S TIP —

This pickle is even better if you make it a few days ahead.

5 Add the vegetables to the sauce. Slowly bring to the boil and allow to cook for 5–10 minutes. Do not overcook – the vegetables should still be crunchy.

6 Add the peanuts and cool. Spoon into clean jars with lids.

Tomato Sambal

Sambal Tomaat, from Surabaya, can be used as a dip to eat with fritters and snack foods.

INGREDIENTS

Makes about 300ml/¹/₂ pint/1¹/₄ cups
2 large beefsteak tomatoes, about
   400g/14oz, peeled if you like
1 fresh red chilli, seeded, or 2.5ml/
   ¹/₂ tsp chilli powder
2–3 garlic cloves
60ml/4 tbsp dark brown sugar
45ml/3 tbsp sunflower oil
15ml/1 tbsp lime or lemon juice
salt

1 Cut the tomatoes in quarters and remove the cores. Place in a food processor, with the chilli or chilli powder, garlic, sugar and salt to taste. Process to a purée.

2 Fry the tomato pureé in hot oil, stirring all the time, until the mixture thickens and has lost its raw taste. Add the lime or lemon juice. Cool, then season. Serve warm or col◀

Carrot and Apple Salad

Known as *Selada Bortel*, this simple, crunchy salad is always a perfect accompaniment to spicy Indonesian food. It's best to grate the apple at the last minute and sprinkle it liberally with lemon juice to prevent discoloration. Cover the salad with clear film and store in the fridge until needed.

INGREDIENTS

Serves 6
3 large carrots
1 green apple
juice of 1 lemon
45ml/3 tbsp sunflower oil
5ml/1 tsp sugar
salt and freshly ground black pepper

1 Coarsely grate the carrot and set aside. Grate the apple, including the skin and drizzle it with the lemon juice to prevent discolouration. Mix gently with your hand to evenly coat the apple with the lemon juice.

2 Add the sunflower oil and sugar t◀ the apple mixture. Season to taste with salt and black pepper, then stir in the grated carrot.

3 Cover the salad with clear film an◀ chill in the fridge for a short time, until required.

 VARIATION ———

For a tangy flavour, add lime juice and a little grated lime rind to the apple.

Sweet and Sour Fruit and Vegetable Salad

Acar Bening makes a perfect accompaniment to many spicy dishes, with its clean taste and bright, jewel-like colours. Any leftover salad can be covered and stored in the fridge for up to two days. This is an essential dish for buffets when it will be enough for about eight servings.

INGREDIENTS

Serves 8

1 small cucumber
1 onion, thinly sliced and sprinkled with salt
1 small, ripe pineapple or 425g/15oz can pineapple rings
1 green pepper, seeded and thinly sliced
3 firm tomatoes, cut in wedges
25g/1oz golden granulated sugar
45–60ml/3–4 tbsp cider or white wine vinegar
120ml/4fl oz/½ cup water
salt

1 Peel the cucumber and cut in half lengthways. Remove the seeds with a small spoon. Cut the cucumber in even-size pieces. Sprinkle with a little salt. Rinse and dry the onion and place in a large bowl. Rinse the cucumber and pat dry, then add to the onion in the bowl.

2 Peel the fresh pineapple, if using, removing all the eyes by cutting them out from top to bottom. Slice the pineapple thinly, then core the slices and cut in neat pieces. If using canned pineapple rings, cut in similarly sized pieces. Add them to the bowl together with the green pepper and tomatoes.

3 Heat the sugar, vinegar and water until the sugar dissolves. Remove from the heat and leave to cool. When cold, add a little salt to taste and then pour over the fruit and vegetables. Cover and chill until required.

--- VARIATION ---

To make an Indonesian-style Cucumber Salad, prepare a whole cucumber as in the above recipe. Make half the dressing and pour over the cucumber. Add a few chopped spring onions. Cover and chill. Serve scattered with toasted sesame seeds.

Chilli Sambal

Sambal Ulek will keep for several weeks in a well-sealed jar in the fridge, so it is worth making up a reasonable quantity at a time. Use a stainless-steel or plastic spoon to measure it out. This sauce is fiercely hot and, should you get any on your fingers, wash them well in soapy water *immediately*.

INGREDIENTS

Makes 450g/1lb

450g/1lb fresh red chillies, seeded
10ml/2 tsp salt

1 Plunge the chillies into a pan of boiling water and cook for 5–8 minutes. Drain and then grind in a food processor, without making the paste too smooth.

2 Turn into a screw-topped glass jar, stir in the salt and cover with a piece of greaseproof paper or clear film. Then screw on the lid and store in the fridge. Spoon into small dishes, to serve as an accompaniment, or use in recipes as suggested.

RICE
AND
NOODLES

Rice is served in Indonesia at least once, and more
often twice, a day. Even today, many people from
the city will return home to help their families and
neighbours with the rice harvest. Lebaran, the
feast day to celebrate the end of Ramadan, is the
time when all families come together and a huge,
cone-shaped mound of Nasi Kuning or Festive
Rice, is the centrepiece of the table.
Noodles, mee, reflect the Chinese influence on
Indonesian cuisine and variations of these recipes
will be found in many neighbouring countries.

Noodles, Chicken and Prawns in Coconut Broth

INGREDIENTS

Serves 8
2 onions, quartered
2.5cm/1in fresh root ginger, sliced
2 garlic cloves
4 macadamia nuts or 8 almonds
1–2 fresh chillies, seeded and sliced
2 lemon grass stems, lower 5cm/
    2in sliced
5cm/2in fresh turmeric, peeled and
    sliced, or 5ml/1 tsp ground turmeric
15ml/1 tbsp coriander seeds, dry-fried
5ml/1 tsp cumin seeds, dry-fried
60ml/4 tbsp sunflower oil
400ml/14fl oz can coconut milk
1.5 litres/2½ pints/6¼ cups stock
375g/13oz packet rice noodles, soaked
    in cold water
350g/12oz cooked tiger prawns
salt and freshly ground black pepper

For the garnishes
4 hard-boiled eggs
225g/8oz cooked chicken, chopped
225g/8oz beansprouts
1 bunch spring onions, shredded
Deep-fried Onions

1 Place the quartered onions, ginger, garlic and nuts in a food processor with the chillies, sliced lemon grass, and turmeric. Process to a paste. Alternatively, pound all the ingredients with a pestle in a mortar. Grind the coriander and cumin seeds coarsely and add to the paste.

2 Heat the oil in a pan and fry the spice paste, without colouring, to bring out the flavours. Add the coconut milk, stock and seasoning. Simmer for 5–10 minutes, while preparing the noodles and garnishes.

3 Drain the noodles and plunge them into a large pan of salted, boiling water for 2 minutes. Remove from the heat and drain in a colander. Rinse well with plenty of cold water, to halt the cooking. Add the tiger prawns to the soup just before serving and heat through for a minute or two.

4 Shell the hard-boiled eggs and cut into quarters. Arrange the garnishes in separate bowls. Each person helps themselves to noodles, tops them with soup, eggs, chicken or beansprouts then scatters shredded spring onions and Deep-fried Onions on top.

Compressed-rice Shapes

INGREDIENTS

Serves 4–8
2 x 115g/4oz packets boil-in-the-
    bag rice
salt

--- COOK'S TIP ---

For the best results for *Longtong*, use boil-in-the-bag rice that is not marked as par-boiled. The grains need to compress and stick together to make the rice cakes, and par-boiled rice grains remain too separate. Otherwise use Basmati or Thai fragrant rice and wrap in muslin bags or foil. Traditionally, these packets are made from banana leaves or woven coconut fronds.

2 Lift out the bags of rice, drain and leave to cool completely, before stripping off the bags.

1 Place the bags of rice in a large pan of salted, boiling water and cook for 1¼ hours, or until the rice is cooked and fills the whole bag like a plump cushion. The bags must be covered with water throughout; use a saucer or plate to weigh them down.

3 With a sharp, wetted knife, cut into neat cubes or slices and then into diamond shapes. Serve with *satés*.

Festive Rice

Nasi Kuning is served at special events – weddings, birthdays or farewell parties.

INGREDIENTS

Serves 8

450g/1lb Thai fragrant rice
60ml/4 tbsp oil
2 garlic cloves, crushed
2 onions, finely sliced
5cm/2in fresh turmeric, peeled
  and crushed
750ml/1¼ pints/3 cups water
400ml/14fl oz can coconut milk
1–2 lemon grass stems, bruised
1–2 *pandan* leaves (optional)
salt

For the accompaniments

omelette strips
2 fresh red chillies, shredded
cucumber chunks
tomato wedges
Deep-fried Onions
Coconut and Peanut Relish (optional)
Prawn Crackers

1 Wash the rice in several changes of water. Drain well.

2 Heat the oil in a wok and gently fry the crushed garlic, the finely sliced onions and the crushed fresh turmeric for a few minutes until soft but not browned.

──────── COOK'S TIP ────────

It is the custom to shape the rice into a cone (to represent a volcano) and then surround with the accompaniments. Shape with oiled hands or use a conical sieve.

3 Add the rice and and stir well so that each grain is thoroughly coated. Pour in the water and coconut milk and add the lemon grass, *pandan* leaves, if using, and salt.

4 Bring to the boil, stirring well. Cover and cook gently for about 15–20 minutes, until all of the liquid has been absorbed.

5 Remove from the heat. Cover with a dish towel, put on the lid and leave to stand in a warm place, for 15 minutes. Remove the lemon grass and *pandan* leaves.

6 Turn on to a serving platter and garnish with the accompaniments.

Nasi Goreng

One of the most familiar and well-known Indonesian dishes. This is a marvellous way to use up leftover rice, chicken and meats such as pork. It is important that the rice is quite cold and the grains separate before adding the other ingredients, so it's best to cook the rice the day before.

INGREDIENTS

Serves 4–6

350g/12oz dry weight long-grain rice, such as basmati, cooked and allowed to become completely cold
2 eggs
30ml/2 tbsp water
105ml/7 tbsp oil
225g/8oz pork fillet or fillet of beef
115g/4oz cooked, peeled prawns
175–225g/6–8oz cooked chicken, chopped
2–3 fresh red chillies, seeded and sliced
1cm/½in cube *terasi*
2 garlic cloves, crushed
1 onion, sliced
30ml/2 tbsp dark soy sauce or 45–60ml/3–4 tbsp tomato ketchup
salt and freshly ground black pepper
celery leaves, Deep-fried Onions and coriander sprigs, to garnish

2 Beat the eggs with seasoning and the water and make two or three omelettes in a frying pan, with a minimum of oil. Roll up each omelette and cut in strips when cold. Set aside.

3 Cut the pork or beef into neat strips and put the meat, prawns and chicken pieces in separate bowls. Shred one of the chillies and reserve it.

1 Once the rice is cooked and cooled, fork it through to separate the grains and keep it in a covered pan or dish until required.

4 Put the *terasi*, with the remaining chilli, garlic and onion, in a food processor and grind to a fine paste. Alternatively, pound together using a pestle and mortar.

5 Fry the paste in the remaining hot oil, without browning, until it gives off a rich, spicy aroma. Add the pork or beef, tossing the meat all the time, to seal in the juices. Cook for 2 minutes, stirring constantly. Add the prawns, cook for 2 minutes and then stir in the chicken, cold rice, dark soy sauce or ketchup and seasoning to taste. Stir all the time to keep the rice light and fluffy and prevent it from sticking.

6 Turn on to a hot platter and garnish with the omelette strips, celery leaves, onions, reserved shredded chilli and the coriander sprigs.

Coconut Rice

This is a very popular way of cooking rice throughout the whole of south-east Asia. *Nasi Uduk* makes a wonderful accompaniment to any dish, and goes particularly well with fish, chicken and pork.

INGREDIENTS

Serves 4–6

350g/12oz Thai fragrant rice
400ml/14fl oz can coconut milk
300ml/½ pint/1¼ cups water
2.5ml/½ tsp ground coriander
1 cinnamon stick
1 lemon grass stem, bruised
1 *pandan* or bay leaf (optional)
salt
Deep-fried Onions, to garnish

1 Wash the rice in several changes of water and then put in a pan with the coconut milk, water, coriander, cinnamon stick, lemon grass and *pandan* or bay leaf, if using, and salt. Bring to the boil, stirring to prevent the rice from settling on the base of the pan. Cover and cook over a very low heat for 12–15 minutes, or until all the coconut milk has been absorbed.

2 Fork the rice through carefully and remove the cinnamon stick, lemon grass and *pandan* or bay leaf. Cover the pan with a tight-fitting lid and then cook over the lowest possible heat for a further 3–5 minutes.

3 Pile the rice on to a warm serving dish and serve garnished with the crisp Deep-fried Onions.

Rice Porridge with Chicken

Bubur Ayam is a dish which pops up all over the East, often served as sustaining breakfast fare. It can be served very simply, with just the chicken stirred into it. Hearty eaters tuck into helpings of porridge drizzled with a little soy sauce, with strips of chicken, prawns, Deep-fried Onions, garlic and strips of fresh chilli, topped with a lightly fried egg and garnished with celery leaves.

INGREDIENTS

Serves 6

1kg/2¼ lb chicken, cut in 4 pieces or 4 chicken quarters
1.75 litres/3 pints/7½ cups water
1 large onion, quartered
2.5cm/1in fresh root ginger, peeled, halved and bruised
350g/12oz Thai fragrant rice, rinsed
salt and freshly ground black pepper

1 Place the chicken pieces in a large pan with the water, onion quarters and ginger. Add seasoning, bring to the boil and then simmer for 45–50 minutes, until the chicken is tender. Remove from the heat. Lift out the chicken, remove the meat and discard the skin and bones. Cut the chicken into bite-size pieces. Reserve the stock.

2 Strain the chicken stock into a clean pan and make it up to 1.75 litres/3 pints/7½ cups with water.

3 Add the rinsed rice to the chicken stock and stir continuously until it comes to the boil, to prevent the rice from settling on the base of the pan. Simmer gently for 20 minutes, without a lid. Stir, cover and cook for a further 20 minutes, stirring from time to time until the rice is soft and rather like a creamy risotto.

4 Stir the chicken pieces into the porridge and heat through for 5 minutes. Serve as it is, or with any of the garnishes and accompaniments suggested in the introduction.

Noodles with Meatballs

Mie Rebus is a one-pot meal, for which the East is renowned. It's fast food, served from street stalls.

INGREDIENTS

Serves 6

450g/1lb Spicy Meatball mixture
350g/12oz dried egg noodles
45ml/3 tbsp sunflower oil
1 large onion, finely sliced
2 garlic cloves, crushed
2.5cm/1in fresh root ginger, peeled
    and cut in thin matchsticks
1.2 litres/2 pints/5 cups stock
30ml/2 tbsp dark soy sauce
2 celery sticks, finely sliced,
    leaves reserved
6 Chinese leaves, cut in bite-size pieces
1 handful mange-touts, cut in strips
salt and freshly ground black pepper

1 Prepare the meatballs, making them quite small. Set aside.

2 Add the noodles to a large pan of salted, boiling water and stir so that the noodles do not settle at the bottom. Simmer for 3–4 minutes, or until *al dente*. Drain in a colander and rinse with plenty of cold water. Set aside.

3 Heat the oil in a wide pan and fry the onion, garlic and ginger until soft but not browned. Add the stock and soy sauce and bring to the boil.

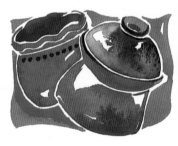

4 Add the meatballs, half-cover and allow to simmer until they are cooked, about 5–8 minutes depending on size. Just before serving, add the sliced celery and, after 2 minutes, add the Chinese leaves and mange-touts. Taste and adjust the seasoning.

5 Divide the noodles among soup bowls, add the meatballs and vegetables and pour the soup on top. Garnish with the reserved celery leaves.

Bamie Goreng

This fried noodle dish is wonderfully accommodating. To the basic recipe you can add other vegetables, such as mushrooms, tiny pieces of chayote, broccoli, leeks or beansprouts, if you prefer. As with fried rice, you can use whatever you have to hand, bearing in mind the need to achieve a balance of colours, flavours and textures.

INGREDIENTS

Serves 6–8

450g/1lb dried egg noodles
1 boneless, skinless chicken breast
115g/4oz pork fillet
115g/4oz calves' liver (optional)
2 eggs, beaten
90ml/6 tbsp oil
25g/1oz butter or margarine
2 garlic cloves, crushed
115g/4oz cooked, peeled prawns
115g/4oz spinach or Chinese leaves
2 celery sticks, finely sliced
4 spring onions, shredded
about 60ml/4 tbsp chicken stock
dark soy sauce and light soy sauce
salt and freshly ground black pepper
Deep-fried Onions and celery leaves,
    to garnish
Sweet and Sour Fruit and Vegetable
    Salad, to serve (optional)

1 Cook the noodles in salted, boiling water for 3–4 minutes. Drain, rinse with cold water and drain again. Set aside until required.

2 Finely slice the chicken, pork fillet and calves' liver, if using.

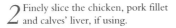

3 Season the eggs. Heat 5ml/1 tsp oil with the butter or margarine in a small pan until melted and then stir in the eggs and keep stirring until scrambled. Set aside.

4 Heat the remaining oil in a wok and fry the garlic with the chicken, pork and liver for 2–3 minutes, until they have changed colour. Add the prawns, spinach or Chinese leaves, celery and spring onions, tossing well.

5 Add the cooked and drained noodles and toss well again so that all the ingredients are well mixed. Add enough stock just to moisten and dark and light soy sauce to taste. Finally, stir in the scrambled eggs.

6 Garnish the dish with Deep-fried Onions and celery leaves. Serve with Sweet and Sour Fruit and Vegetable Salad, if using.

VEGETABLES
AND SALADS

Gado-gado, *along with* satés *and Rendang, has
gained an international reputation – and
rightly so. Presentation is all important –
try serving a platter of the lightly-blanched
vegetables or fruit and raw vegetables, each with
peanut sauce, as a stunning lunch dish. Other
vegetables, from Stir-fried Greens and the delicious
Spiced Cauliflower Braise to the steamed
Courgettes with Noodles dish, illustrate the rich
variety of vegetarian-style Indonesian recipes that
are on hand to tempt you.*

Spiced Cauliflower Braise

A delicious vegetable stew, known as *Sambal Kol Kembang,* which combines coconut milk with spices and is perfect as a vegetarian main course or as part of a buffet.

INGREDIENTS

Serves 4
1 cauliflower
2 medium or 1 large tomato(es)
1 onion, chopped
2 garlic cloves, crushed
1 fresh green chilli, seeded
2.5ml/¹/₂ tsp ground turmeric
1cm/¹/₂ in cube *terasi*
30ml/2 tbsp sunflower oil
400ml/14fl oz coconut milk
250ml/8fl oz/1 cup water
5ml/1 tsp sugar
5ml/1 tsp tamarind pulp, soaked in
    45ml/3 tbsp warm water
salt

1 Trim the stalk from the cauliflower and divide into tiny florets. Skin the tomato(es) if liked. Chop the flesh into 1–2.5cm/¹/₂–1in pieces.

2 Grind the chopped onion, garlic, green chilli, ground turmeric and *terasi* together to a paste in a food processor or with a pestle and mortar. Heat the sunflower oil in a wok or large frying pan and fry the spice paste to bring out the aromatic flavours, without allowing it to brown.

3 Add the cauliflower florets and toss well to coat in the spices. Stir in the coconut milk, water, sugar and salt to taste. Simmer for 5 minutes. Strain the tamarind and reserve the juice.

4 Add the tamarind juice and chopped tomatoes to the pan then cook for 2–3 minutes only. Taste and check the seasoning and serve.

Spicy Scrambled Eggs

This is a lovely way to liven up scrambled eggs. When making *Orak Arik,* prepare all the ingredients ahead so that the vegetables retain all their crunch and colour.

INGREDIENTS

Serves 4
30ml/2 tbsp sunflower oil
1 onion, finely sliced
225g/8oz Chinese leaves, finely sliced
    or cut in diamonds
200g/7oz can sweetcorn kernels
1 small fresh red chilli, seeded and
    finely sliced (optional)
30ml/2 tbsp water
2 eggs, beaten
salt and freshly ground black pepper
Deep-fried Onions, to garnish

1 Heat a wok, add the oil and fry the onion, until soft but not browned.

2 Add the Chinese leaves and toss well together. Add the sweetcorn, chilli and water. Cover with a lid and cook for 2 minutes.

3 Remove the lid and stir in the beaten eggs and seasoning. Stir constantly until the eggs are creamy and just set. Serve on warmed plates, scattered with crisp Deep-fried Onions

Tomato and Onion Salad

A refreshing salad, *Atjar Ketimun,* which can be made ahead; it improves if well chilled before serving. Use firm, slightly under-ripe tomatoes so the flesh does not collapse when cut into dice.

INGREDIENTS

Serves 6

1 cucumber
45ml/3 tbsp good-quality rice or white
   wine vinegar
10ml/2 tsp sugar
1 tomato, skinned, seeded and diced
1 small onion, finely sliced
1 fresh red chilli, seeded and chopped
salt

1 Trim the ends from the cucumber. Peel it lengthways but leave some of the skin on, to make the salad look more attractive. Cut it in thin slices and lay them out on a large plate. Sprinkle with a little salt and leave for 15 minutes. Rinse well and dry.

2 Mix the vinegar, sugar and a pinch of salt together. Arrange all the vegetables in a bowl and pour over the vinegar, sugar and salt mixture. Cover the salad and chill before serving.

Coconut and Peanut Relish

The aroma of toasted coconut is wonderful and immediately will have you dreaming of warmer climes! *Serudeng* is served as an accompaniment to many Indonesian dishes; any leftovers can be stored in an airtight tin.

INGREDIENTS

Serves 6–8

115g/4oz fresh coconut, grated, or
   desiccated coconut
175g/6oz salted peanuts
5mm/¼ in cube *terasi*
1 small onion, quartered
2–3 garlic cloves, crushed
45ml/3 tbsp oil
2.5ml/½ tsp tamarind pulp, soaked in
   30ml/2 tbsp warm water
5ml/1 tsp coriander seeds, dry-fried
   and ground
2.5ml/½ tsp cumin seeds, dry-fried
   and ground
5ml/1 tsp dark brown sugar

1 Dry-fry the coconut in a wok or large frying pan over a medium heat, turning *all the time,* until crisp and a rich, golden colour. Allow to cool and add half to the peanuts. Toss together to mix.

2 Grind the *terasi,* with the onion and garlic, to a paste in a food processor or with a pestle and mortar. Fry in hot oil, without browning. Strain the tamarind and reserve the juice. Add the coriander, cumin, tamarind juice and brown sugar to the fried paste. Stir all the time and cook for 2–3 minutes.

3 Stir in the remaining toasted coconut and leave to cool. When quite cold, mix with the peanut and coconut mixture.

Bean Curd and Cucumber Salad

Tahu Goreng Ketjap is a nutritious and refreshing salad with a hot, sweet and sour dressing. It is ideal for buffets.

INGREDIENTS

Serves 4–6

1 small cucumber
oil for frying
1 square fresh or 115g/4oz long-life
  bean curd
115g/4oz beansprouts, trimmed
  and rinsed
salt

For the dressing

1 small onion, grated
2 garlic cloves, crushed
5–7.5ml/1–1½ tsp Chilli Sambal
30–45ml/2–3 tbsp dark soy sauce
15–30ml/1–2 tbsp rice-wine vinegar
10ml/2 tsp dark brown sugar
salt
celery leaves, to garnish

1 Trim the ends from the cucumber and then cut it in neat cubes. Sprinkle with salt and set aside, while preparing the remaining ingredients.

— COOK'S TIP —

Beansprouts come from the mung bean and are easily grown at home on damp cotton or in a plastic bean sprouter. They must be eaten when absolutely fresh, so when buying from a shop check that they are crisp and are not beginning to go brown or soft. Eat within a day or two.

2 Heat a little oil in a pan and fry the bean curd on both sides until golden brown. Drain on absorbent kitchen paper and cut in cubes.

3 Prepare the dressing by blending together the onion, garlic and Chilli Sambal. Stir in the soy sauce, vinegar, sugar and salt to taste. You can do this in a screw-topped glass jar.

4 Just before serving, rinse the cucumber under cold running water. Drain and dry thoroughly. Toss the cucumber, bean curd and beansprouts together in a serving bowl and pour over the dressing. Garnish with the celery leaves and serve the salad at once.

Stir-fried Greens

Quail's eggs look very attractive in *Chah Kang Kung*, but you can substitute some baby sweetcorn, halved at an angle.

INGREDIENTS

Serves 4

2 bunches spinach or chard or 1 head
    Chinese leaves or 450g/1lb curly kale
3 garlic cloves, crushed
5cm/2in fresh root ginger, peeled and
    cut in matchsticks
45–60ml/3–4 tbsp groundnut oil
115g/4oz boneless, skinless chicken
    breast, or pork fillet, or a mixture of
    both, very finely sliced
12 quail's eggs, hard-boiled and shelled
1 fresh red chilli, seeded and shredded
30–45ml/2–3 tbsp oyster sauce
15ml/1 tbsp brown sugar
10ml/2 tsp cornflour, mixed with
    50ml/2fl oz/¼ cup cold water
salt

—————— COOK'S TIP ——————

As with all stir-fries, don't start cooking until you have prepared all the ingredients and arranged them to hand. Cut everything into small, even-size pieces so the food can be cooked very quickly and all the colours and flavours preserved.

1 Wash the chosen leaves well and shake them dry. Strip the tender leaves from the stems and tear them into pieces. Discard the lower, tougher part of the stems and slice the remainder evenly.

2 Fry the garlic and ginger in the hot oil, without browning, for a minute. Add the chicken and/or pork and keep stirring it in the wok until the meat changes colour. When the meat looks cooked, add the sliced stems first and cook them quickly; then add the torn leaves, quail's eggs and chilli. Spoon in the oyster sauce and a little boiling water, if necessary. Cover and cook for 1–2 minutes only.

3 Remove the cover, stir and add sugar and salt to taste. Stir in the cornflour and water mixture and toss thoroughly. Cook until the mixture is well coated in a glossy sauce.

4 Serve immediately, while still very hot and the colours are bright and positively jewel-like.

Indonesian Potatoes with Onions and Chilli Sauce

This adds another dimension to potato chips, with the addition of crisply fried onions and a hot soy sauce and chilli dressing. Eat *Kentang Gula* hot, warm or cold, as a tasty snack.

INGREDIENTS

Serves 6
3 large potatoes, about 225g/8oz each, peeled and cut into chips
sunflower or groundnut oil for deep-frying
2 onions, finely sliced
salt

For the dressing
1–2 fresh red chillies, seeded and ground, or 2.5ml/½ tsp Chilli Sambal
45ml/3 tbsp dark soy sauce

1 Rinse the potato chips and then pat dry very well with kitchen paper. Heat the oil and deep-fry the chips, until they are golden brown in colour and crisp.

2 Put the chips in a dish, sprinkle with salt and keep warm. Fry the onion slices in the hot oil until they are similarly crisp and golden brown. Drain well on kitchen paper and then add to the potato chips.

3 Mix the chillies or Chilli Sambal with the soy sauce and heat gently.

4 Pour over the potato and onion mixture and serve as suggested.

--- VARIATION ---

Alternatively, boil the potatoes in their skins. Drain, cool and slice them and then shallow-fry until golden. Cook the onions and pour over the dressing, as above.

Courgettes with Noodles

Any courgette or member of the squash family can be used in *Oseng Oseng,* which is very similar to a dish enjoyed in Malaysia, whose cuisine has strong links with Indonesia.

INGREDIENTS

Serves 4–6
450g/1lb courgettes, sliced
1 onion, finely sliced
1 garlic clove, finely chopped
30ml/2 tbsp sunflower oil
2.5ml/½ tsp ground turmeric
2 tomatoes, chopped
45ml/3 tbsp water
115g/4oz cooked, peeled prawns (optional)
25g/1oz cellophane noodles
salt

1 Use a potato peeler to cut thin strips from the outside of each courgette. Cut them in neat slices. Set the courgettes on one side. Fry the onion and garlic in hot oil; do not allow to brown.

2 Add the turmeric, courgette slices, chopped tomatoes, water and prawns, if using.

3 Put the noodles in a pan and pour over boiling water to cover, leave for a minute and then drain. Cut the noodles in 5cm/2in lengths and add to the vegetables.

4 Cover with a lid and cook in their own steam for 2–3 minutes. Toss everything well together. Season with salt to taste and serve while still hot.

Cooked Vegetable Gado-Gado

Instead of putting everything on a large platter, you can serve individual servings of this salad. It is a perfect recipe for lunchtime or informal gatherings.

INGREDIENTS

Serves 6
225g/8oz waxy potatoes, cooked
450g/1lb mixed cabbage, spinach and
  beansprouts, in equal proportions,
  rinsed and shredded
½ cucumber, cut in wedges, salted and
  set aside for 15 minutes
2–3 eggs, hard-boiled and shelled
115g/4oz fresh bean curd
oil for frying
6–8 large Prawn Crackers
lemon juice
Deep-fried Onions, to garnish
Peanut Sauce, to serve

1 Cube the potatoes and set aside. Bring a large pan of salted water to the boil. Plunge one type of raw vegetable at a time into the pan for just a few seconds to blanch. Lift out the vegetables with a large draining spoon or sieve and run under very cold water. Or plunge them into iced water and leave for 2 minutes. Drain thoroughly. Blanch all the vegetables, except the cucumber, in this way.

2 Rinse the cucumber pieces and drain them well. Cut the eggs in quarters. Cut the bean curd into cubes.

3 Fry the bean curd in hot oil in a wok until crisp on both sides. Lift out and drain on kitchen paper.

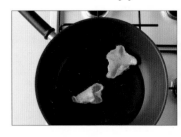

4 Add more oil to the pan and then deep-fry the Prawn Crackers one or two at a time. Reserve them on a tray lined with kitchen paper.

5 Arrange all the cooked vegetables attractively on a platter, with the cucumber, hard-boiled eggs and bean curd. Scatter with the lemon juice and Deep-fried Onions at the last minute.

6 Serve with the prepared Peanut Sauce and hand round the fried Prawn Crackers separately.

Fruit and Raw Vegetable Gado-Gado

A banana leaf, which can be bought from oriental stores, can be used to line the platter for a special occasion.

INGREDIENTS

Serves 6

2 unripe pears, peeled at the last moment, or 175g/6oz wedge *bangkuang* (yambean), peeled and cut in matchsticks
1–2 eating apples
juice of ½ lemon
1 small, crisp lettuce, shredded
½ cucumber, seeded, sliced and salted, set aside for 15 minutes, then rinsed and drained
6 small tomatoes, cut in wedges
3 slices fresh pineapple, cored and cut in wedges
3 eggs or 12 quail's eggs, hard-boiled and shelled
175g/6oz egg noodles, cooked, cooled and chopped
Deep-fried Onions, to garnish

Peanut Sauce

2–4 fresh red chillies, seeded and ground, or 15ml/1 tbsp Chilli Sambal
300ml/½ pint/1¼ cups coconut milk
350g/12oz crunchy peanut butter
15ml/1 tbsp dark soy sauce or dark brown sugar
5ml/1 tsp tamarind pulp, soaked in 45ml/3 tbsp warm water, strained and juice reserved
coarsely crushed peanuts
salt

1 To make the Peanut Sauce, put the chillies or Chilli Sambal and coconut milk in a pan. Add the peanut butter and heat gently, stirring, until no lumps of peanut butter remain.

2 Allow to simmer gently until the sauce thickens, then add the soy sauce or sugar and tamarind juice. Season with salt to taste. Pour into a bowl and sprinkle with a few coarsely crushed peanuts.

3 To make the salad, peel and core the pears or *bangkuang* and apples. Slice the apples and sprinkle with lemon juice. Arrange the salad and fruit attractively on a flat platter. The lettuce can be used, instead of a banana leaf, to form a bed for the salad.

4 Add the sliced or quartered hard-boiled eggs (leave quail's eggs whole), the chopped noodles and the Deep-fried Onions.

5 Serve at once, accompanied with a bowl of the Peanut Sauce.

DESSERTS

Desserts do not normally have a high profile on the Indonesian menu; fresh fruit is so abundant that this would be the usual choice after a large buffet meal. However, here is a small sample of firm favourites. The Deep-fried Bananas are so popular you can buy them from the warungs *(street vendors). They are hard to beat when freshly cooked. Do try the Black Glutinous Rice Pudding; it is a unique and delicious experience.*

Black Glutinous Rice Pudding

This very unusual rice pudding, *Bubor Pulot Hitam,* which uses bruised fresh root ginger, is quite delicious. When cooked, black rice still retains its husk and has a nutty texture. Serve in small bowls, with a little coconut cream poured over each helping.

INGREDIENTS

Serves 6
115g/4oz black glutinous rice
475ml/16fl oz/2 cups water
1cm/½ in fresh root ginger, peeled
    and bruised
50g/2oz dark brown sugar
50g/2oz caster sugar
300ml/½ pint/1¼ cups coconut milk
    or cream, to serve

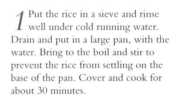

1 Put the rice in a sieve and rinse well under cold running water. Drain and put in a large pan, with the water. Bring to the boil and stir to prevent the rice from settling on the base of the pan. Cover and cook for about 30 minutes.

2 Add the ginger and both the brown and caster sugar. Cook for a further 15 minutes, adding a little more water if necessary, until the rice is cooked and porridge-like. Remove the ginger and serve warm, in bowls, topped with coconut milk or cream.

Deep-fried Bananas

Known as *Pisang Goreng,* these delicious deep-fried bananas should be cooked at the last minute, so that the outer crust of batter is crisp in texture and the banana is soft and warm inside.

INGREDIENTS

Serves 8
115g/4oz self-raising flour
40g/1½oz rice flour
2.5ml/½ tsp salt
200ml/7fl oz /scant 1 cup water
finely grated lime rind (optional)
8 small bananas
oil for deep-frying
sugar and 1 lime, cut in wedges,
    to serve

1 Sift both the flours and the salt together into a bowl. Add just enough water to make a smooth, coating batter. Mix well, then add the lime rind, if using.

2 Peel the bananas and dip them into the batter two or three times.

3 Heat the oil to 190°C/375°F or when a cube of day-old bread browns in 30 seconds. Deep-fry the battered bananas until crisp and golden. Drain and serve hot, dredged with sugar and with the lime wedges to squeeze over the bananas.

Pancakes Filled with Sweet Coconut

Traditionally, the pale green colour in the batter for *Dadar Gulung* was obtained from the juice squeezed from *pandan* leaves – a real labour of love. Green food colouring can be used as the modern alternative to this lengthy process.

INGREDIENTS

Makes 12–15 pancakes

175g/6oz dark brown sugar
450ml/15fl oz/scant 2 cups water
1 *pandan* leaf, stripped through with a
  fork and tied into a knot
175g/6oz desiccated coconut
oil for frying
salt

For the pancake batter

225g/8oz plain flour, sifted
2 eggs, beaten
2 drops of edible green food colouring
few drops of vanilla essence
450ml/15fl oz/scant 2 cups water
45ml/3 tbsp groundnut oil

1 Dissolve the sugar in the water with the *pandan* leaf, in a pan over gentle heat, stirring all the time. Increase the heat and allow to boil gently for 3–4 minutes, until the mixture just becomes syrupy. Do not let it caramelize.

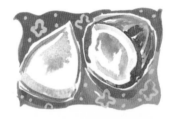

2 Put the coconut into a wok with a pinch of salt. Pour over the prepared sugar syrup and cook over a very gentle heat, stirring from time to time, until the mixture becomes almost dry; this will take 5–10 minutes. Set aside until required.

3 To make the batter, blend together the flour, eggs, food colouring, vanilla essence, water and oil either by hand or in a food processor.

4 Brush an 18cm/7in frying pan with oil and cook 12–15 pancakes. Keep the pancakes warm. Fill each pancake with a generous spoonful of the coconut mixture, roll up and serve them immediately.

Steamed Coconut Custard

Srikaya is a very popular dessert that pops up all over South-east Asia, rather as crème caramel is found all over Europe or, indeed, wherever Europeans have settled.

INGREDIENTS

Serves 8

400ml/14fl oz can coconut milk
75ml/5 tbsp water
25g/1oz sugar
3 eggs, beaten
25g/1oz cellophane noodles, soaked in warm water for 5 minutes
4 ripe bananas or plantains, peeled and cut in small pieces
salt
vanilla ice cream, to serve (optional)

1 Stir the coconut milk, water and sugar into the beaten eggs and whisk well together.

2 Strain into a 1.75 litre/3 pint/7½ cup heatproof soufflé dish.

3 Drain the noodles well and cut them into small pieces with scissors. Stir the noodles into the coconut milk mixture, together with the chopped bananas or plantains. Stir in a pinch of salt.

4 Cover the dish with foil and place in a steamer for about 1 hour, or until set. Test by inserting a thin, small knife or skewer into the centre. Serve hot or cold, on its own or topped with vanilla ice cream.

Index